RESPONSORIAL PSALMS

From the Liturgical Psalter
as used in *The Alternative Service Book 1980*

EDITED BY NORMAN WARREN

HarperCollins*Publishers*
77-85 Fulham Palace Road
Hammersmith
London
W6 8JB

This edition first published in 1994

Compilation copyright © 1994 Norman Warren
Psalm texts from the *The Psalms: a new translation for worship*.
© 1976, 1977 David L Frost, John A Emerton, Andrew A Macintosh

The compiler asserts the moral right to be identified as the compiler of this work.

ISBN 0551 04005 X

Music and text set by Barnes Music Engraving Ltd,
East Sussex, England
Printed and bound in Great Britain by
HarperCollins*Manufacturing*, Glasgow

A catalogue record for this book is available from the British Library.

Photocopying

The Response section **only** may be photocopied free of charge, providing that:

 the copies are used only within a church or other worship service.
b) the copies are not offered for resale in any form.
 copies are used only by the purchasing institution.

roduce items within the book must be sought
dual copyright owners concerned.
dresses appears at the end of the book.

CONTENTS

About the Contributors

Preface

Responsorial Psalms

Responsorial Canticles

Copyright Addresses

Index to Psalm Settings

Index to Psalms for Sundays

Index to Composers

Index to First Lines

About the Contributors

John Barnard is Director of Music at St Alban's Church, North Harrow, and teaches French and German at the John Lyon School, Harrow. Many of his hymn tunes appear in *Hymns for Today's Church*.

Michael Dawney studied under Edmund Rubbra and is a Roman Catholic arranger, editor and composer. He has written music for choir and organ, and contributed to hymn books.

Barry Ferguson studied composition with Herbert Howells, and has spent more than forty years in and around cathedrals, notably those at Exeter, Peterborough and Rochester. Professional engagements have taken him all over the world, and he has recorded and broadcast as singer, organist, pianist, conductor and composer.

Neil Hawes is a music and mathematics graduate now working as a computer consultant. He has written a number of choral pieces including anthems and a communion setting, and is involved in organising the Hounslow Festival of Music, Speech and Dance.

David Iliff is the music editor for *Carols for Today* and *Psalms for Today*. He is now Director of Music at the British School of Brussels.

William Llewellyn founded the Linden singers, and was Director of Music at Charterhouse School from 1965 to 1987. He is the editor of *The Novello Book of Carols* and the Royal School of Church Music's recent publication, *Sing with all my Soul*.

Richard Lloyd was Assistant Organist of Salisbury Cathedral and successively Organist of Hereford and Durham Cathedrals.

Simon Mold is an established composer of church music. He teaches English and Classics in Rochester, and is currently an alto lay clerk at Rochester Cathedral.

Noel Rawsthorne was the Organist of Liverpool Cathedral from 1955 to 1980, and City Organist and Artistic Director of St George's Hall, Liverpool, from 1980 to 1984. He has written many works for church choirs, and published a number of collections of organ music.

Howard Stephens is the Organist and Director of Music at St Mary's Church, Osterley, Middlesex, and the conductor of the St Mary's Singers. He is a composer and arranger, and the Director of the Elbeck Press.

Noël Tredinnick is the Organist and Director of Music at All Souls' Church, Langham Place, and Professor of Conducting at the Guildhall School of Music and Drama. He is a freelance conductor in the UK and USA, particularly of the popular 'Prom Praise' programme and BBC TV's 'Songs of Praise' series.

Norman Warren is the Archdeacon of Rochester and the author of *Journey into Life*. He has contributed to a number of hymnbooks, and was a member of the editorial team for *Hymns for Today's Church* and *Church Family Worship*.

Peter White was until recently the Organist and Master of the Music of Leicester Cathedral.

David Wilson describes himself as 'an entirely amateur composer with the good fortune to get involved with publishing'. He has contributed to *Youth Praise*, *Psalm Praise*, and formed part of the editorial team for *Hymns for Today's Church*.

PREFACE

While many of the most well-known hymns are metrical versions of Psalms, and a number of modern worship songs are also based on the Psalms, the singing of Psalm texts has virtually ceased in many churches today. The chanting of Psalms is mainly a thing of the past except in Cathedrals and parish churches where the traditional Choral Evensong is maintained.

The aim of this book is to bring the singing of Scripture back into worship in all churches, by providing musical settings with Responses which are simple and easy to learn, and require little or no congregational rehearsal. This book contains 97 Responsorial Psalms (one for every Sunday in a two-year cycle), and also includes 10 settings of the Canticles from *The Alternative Service Book 1980*. The musical settings include both chanted Psalms and others in a more free-flowing style.

NOTES ON PERFORMANCE

It is suggested that the organ plays through the Response, and the choir, soloist or music group then sing it in unison. The congregation can repeat the Response, followed by the choir, soloist or music group singing the verses. The Response section may be copied for congregational use under the conditions outlined on p ii.

Generally, the composers have suggested how the verses may be sung, and which voices should be used. However, the verses could also be sung by a single Cantor, and each church may adapt the voices used according to the resources it has available. There are a number of descants for the final Responses. In these cases, the Response is repeated at the end of the Psalm with the descant added, following on directly from the last verse. These settings of Psalms are intended to be a flexible resource capable of being adapted to different voices or instruments, and providing encouragement for local musicians to experiment with their own settings.

ACKNOWLEDGEMENTS

I am especially grateful to Barry Ferguson, Organist and Master of the Choristers at Rochester Cathedral, for his comments and encouragement over the last eighteen months as this project has developed.

This book comes with the prayerful hope:

Let us come before his face with thanksgiving: and cry out to him joyfully in psalms!

(Psalm 95:2)

Norman Warren

PSALM 1: 1–4, 7a

Music: Peter White

RESPONSE

7ª. For the Lord cares for the way of the right - eous.

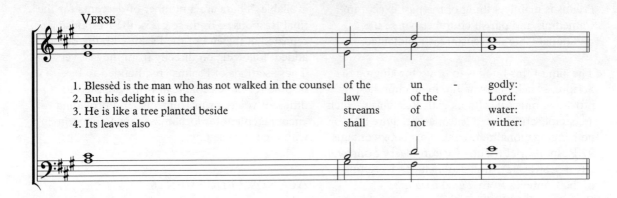

VERSE

1. Blessèd is the man who has not walked in the counsel of the un – godly:
2. But his delight is in the law of the Lord:
3. He is like a tree planted beside streams of water:
4. Its leaves also shall not wither:

(1.) nor followed the way of sinners nor taken his seat a – mongst the scornful.
(2.) and on that law will he pon – der day and night.
(3.) that yields its fruit in due season.
(4.) and look what – ever he does it shall prosper.

PSALM 3: 1–5

Music: Noël Tredinnick

Psalm 7: 7-11

Music: Richard Lloyd

CHOIR (Harmony)

Acc. *mp*

9. Judge for me,__ O Lord,__ ac - cord - ing to__ my

right - eous - ness:__ and as my in - te - gri - ty re - quires.

CHOIR (Unison)

f *dim.* *mp*

10. Let the wick-ed-ness of the un - god - ly cease, but es - tab - lish the right - eous: for

cresc. *dim.*

you try the ve - ry hearts and minds of men, O__ right - eous God.

Psalm 8: 1, 4–7

Music: Norman Warren

RESPONSE

1. O Lord our Gov-er-nor: how glo - rious is your name in all the earth.

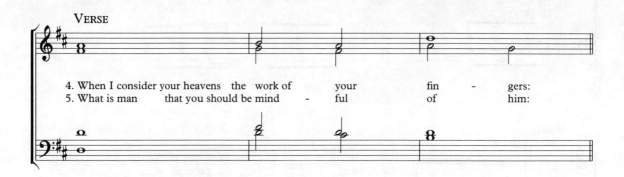

VERSE

4. When I consider your heavens the work of   your   fin - gers:
5. What is man   that you should be mind - ful   of   him:

(4.) the moon and the stars which you   have   set   in_____   or - der.
(5.) or the son of man that   you   should   care   for_____   him?_____

Music: © 1993 Norman Warren / Jubilate Hymns

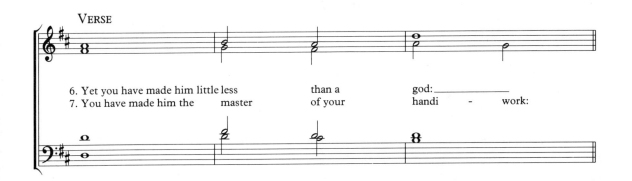

VERSE

6. Yet you have made him little less than a god:
7. You have made him the master of your handi - work:

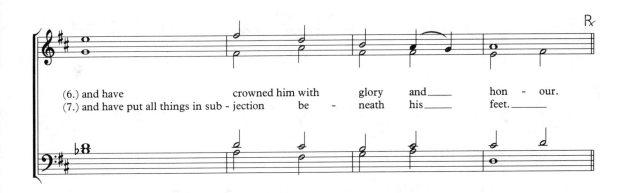

℞

(6.) and have crowned him with glory and hon - our.
(7.) and have put all things in sub - jection be - neath his feet.

RESPONSE (after verse 7)   DESCANT

1. O Lord our Gov-er-nor: how glo - rious is your name in all the earth.

1. O Lord our Gov-er-nor: how glo - rious is your name in all the earth.

Psalm 9: 1, 8–11

Music: Norman Warren

PSALM 10: 13–18a

Music: Peter White

RESPONSE

DESCANT (after verse 17)

Al - le-lu – ia, al - le-lu – ia, al - le-lu-ia, al - le - lu – ia.

18ª. The Lord is king for ev-er and ev-er, for ev-er and ev-er the Lord is king.

Ped.

VERSE
T.B.

13. A - rise O Lord God lift up your hand: for - get not the poor for ev - er.

Man.

VERSE
CHOIR (Harmony)

14. Why should the wicked man spurn God: why should he say in his heart 'He will not a - venge'?

Music: © 1993 Peter White / Jubilate Hymns

VERSE
S.A.

15. Surely you see the trou-ble and the sor-row: you look on and will take it in-to your own hands.

VERSE
CHOIR (Harmony)

16. The helpless commits him-self to you: for you are the help-er of the fa-ther-less.

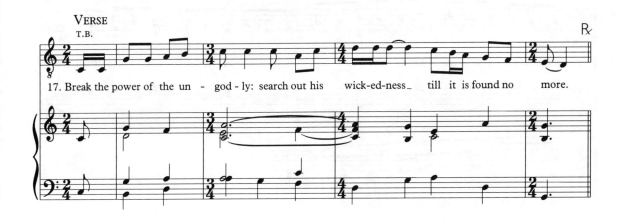

VERSE
T.B.

17. Break the power of the un - god - ly: search out his wick-ed-ness till it is found no more.

PSALM 11: 1–4, 7

Music: Norman Warren

RESPONSE

4. The Lord is in his ho-ly place the Lord is en-throned in heaven.

VERSE
SOLO OR CHOIR (Unison)

1. In the Lord I have found my re-fuge: how then can you say to me

'Flee like a bird to the moun-tains.'

VERSE
SOLO OR CHOIR (Unison)

2. Look how the wick-ed bend their bows and notch the ar-row up-on the string: to

shoot from the dark-ness at the true of heart.

VERSE
SOLO OR CHOIR (Unison)

R

3. 'If the foun-da-tions are___ des-troyed: what can the just___ man do?'___

VERSE
SOLO OR CHOIR (Unison)

7. For the Lord is right - eous and loves right - eous acts: the

up - right shall see___ his face.___

RESPONSE (after verse 7)
DESCANT

4. The Lord is in his ho - ly place the Lord is en - throned in heaven.___

4. The Lord is in his ho - ly place the Lord is en - throned in heaven.___

Psalm 15: 1–7

Music: Norman Warren

Response *verses*

7. They that do_ these things: shall ne-ver be o - ver - thrown.

Verse (vv. 1, 3, 5)

1. Lord who may a - bide in your tabernacle:
3. He that has done no evil to his fellow:
5. He that has sworn to his neighbour:

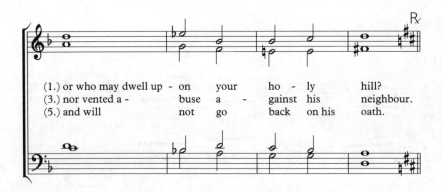

(1.) or who may dwell up - on your ho - ly hill?
(3.) nor vented a - buse a - gainst his neighbour.
(5.) and will not go back on his oath.

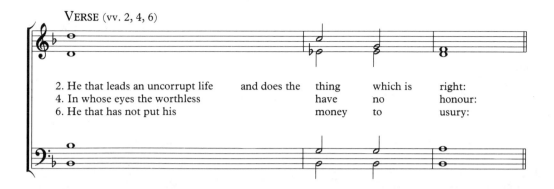

VERSE (vv. 2, 4, 6)

2. He that leads an uncorrupt life   and does the   thing   which is   right:
4. In whose eyes the worthless   have   no   honour:
6. He that has not put his   money   to   usury:

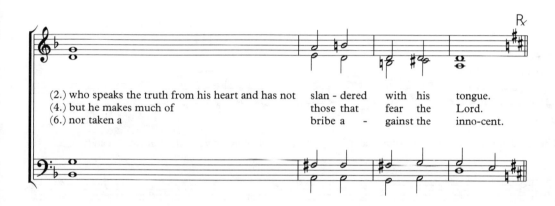

(2.) who speaks the truth from his heart and has not   slan - dered   with his   tongue.
(4.) but he makes much of   those that   fear   the   Lord.
(6.) nor taken a   bribe a   -   gainst the   inno-cent.

RESPONSE (after verse 6)

7. They   that do__ these things: shall   ne-ver be   o - ver - thrown._____

Psalm 16: 1, 5–8

Music: Norman Warren

RESPONSE

1. Pre - serve me O God: in you have I ta - ken re - fuge.___

VERSE
SOLO OR CHOIR (Unison)

5. The Lord is my ap-point-ed por-tion and_ my_ cup: you hold my_ lot_ in your hands.___

VERSE
SOLO OR CHOIR (Unison)

6. The share that has fall-en to me is in plea-sant pla-ces: and a fair land is my pos - ses - sion.___

VERSE
CHOIR (Harmony)

7. I will bless the Lord who has gi-ven me counsel: at night al-so he has in-struc-ted my heart.

VERSE
CHOIR (Harmony)

8. I have set the Lord al - ways be-fore me: he is at my right hand and I shall not fall.

RESPONSE (after verse 8)
DESCANT

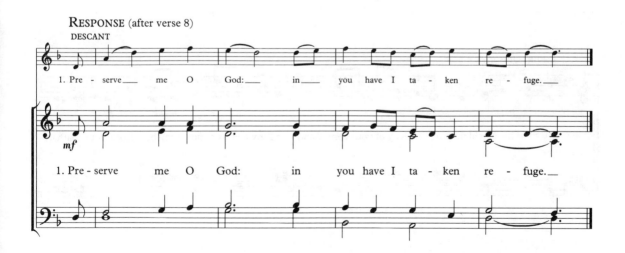

1. Pre - serve me O God: in you have I ta - ken re - fuge.

1. Pre - serve me O God: in you have I ta - ken re - fuge.

Psalm 17: 4–8

Music: Noël Tredinnick

RESPONSE

7ª. Show me the won-ders of your stead-fast love.

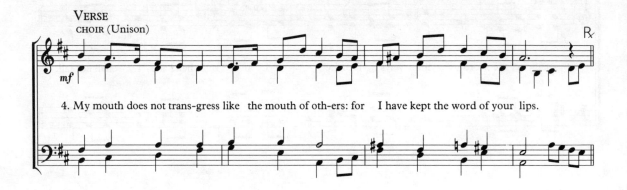

VERSE
CHOIR (Unison)

4. My mouth does not trans-gress like the mouth of oth-ers: for I have kept the word of your lips.

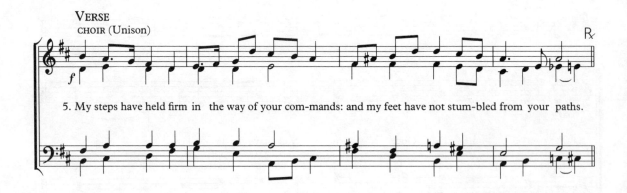

VERSE
CHOIR (Unison)

5. My steps have held firm in the way of your com-mands: and my feet have not stum-bled from your paths.

VERSE
CHOIR (Unison)

6. I call up-on you O God for you will sure-ly an-swer: in-cline your ear to me and hear my words.

VERSE
CHOIR (Unison)

8. Keep me as the ap - ple of your eye: hide me un - der the sha-dow of your wings.

RESPONSE (after verse 8)

7ª. Show me the won-ders of your stead-fast love.

Psalm 18: 1, 32–34

Music: Simon Mold

PSALM 19: 1-6

Music: Norman Warren

Brightly

RESPONSE

1. The hea-vens de-clare the glo-ry of God, and the

fir-ma-ment pro-claims his han - di-work.

vv. 4, 5

VERSE

2. One day tells it to an - oth - er, and night to night com-mu-ni - cates know-ledge.

3. There is no speech or___ lan - guage: nor are their voi - ces heard.

VERSE

T.B.

4. Yet their sound has gone out through all __ the world: and their words to the ends of the earth.

Harmony

5. There he has pitched a __ tent __ for the sun: which comes out as a bride-groom from his

cham-ber and re - joi-ces like a strong man to run __ his __ course. __

S.

6. Its ris-ing is at one end of the hea - vens, and its cir-cuit to their far - thest __

bound: __ and no - thing is hid - den from its heat. __

PSALM 19: 7–10, 14b

Music: Norman Warren

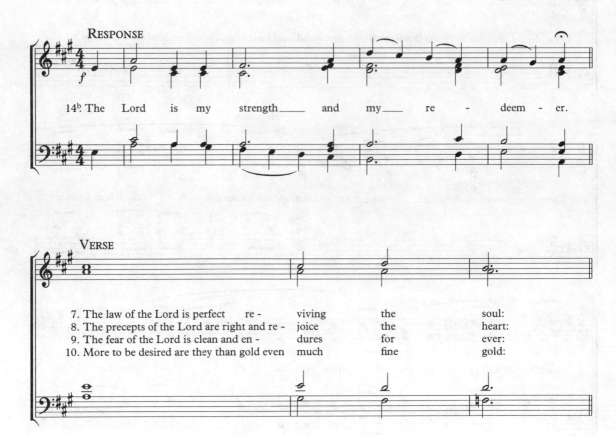

RESPONSE

14b. The Lord is my strength___ and my___ re - deem - er.

VERSE

7. The law of the Lord is perfect re - viving the soul:
8. The precepts of the Lord are right and re - joice the heart:
9. The fear of the Lord is clean and en - dures for ever:
10. More to be desired are they than gold even much fine gold:

Ԗ

(7.) the command of the Lord is true and makes wise the sim - ple.
(8.) the commandment of the Lord is pure and gives light to the eyes.___
(9.) the judgements of the Lord are unchanging and right - eous ev - ery one.___
(10.) sweeter also than honey than the honey that drips from the comb.___

Psalm 20: 1–4, 7b

Music: Michael Dawney

PSALM 22: 23–26, 29

Music: Neil Hawes

RESPONSE

29. For the king-dom is the Lord's: and he shall be ru-ler o-ver the na-tions.

Ped.

VERSE

23. I will tell of your name to my brethren: in the midst of the con - gre - ga - tion will I praise you.

VERSE

24. O praise the Lord all you that fear him: hold him in honour O seed of Jacob

(24.) and let the seed of Isra - el stand in awe of him.

VERSE

mp

25. For he has not des - pised nor ab - horred the_____ poor man in his misery:

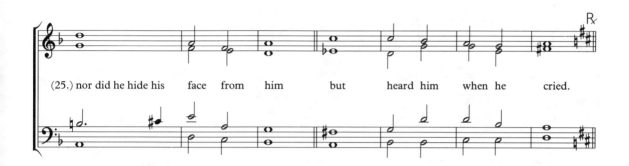

Rx

(25.) nor did he hide his face from him but heard him when he cried.

VERSE

mf

26. From you springs my praise in the great_____ con - gre - gation:

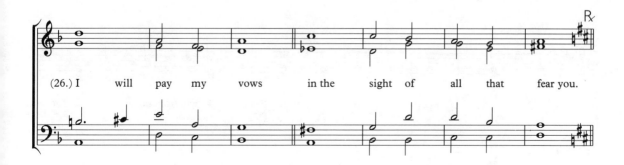

Rx

(26.) I will pay my vows in the sight of all that fear you.

PSALM 23: 1–4, 6

Music: Norman Warren

RESPONSE

1. The Lord is my shep-herd: there-fore can I lack__ no - thing,____

vv. 3, 4, 6

there - fore can I lack__ no - thing.

VERSE
s.

2. He will make me lie down in green pas-tures: and lead me be - side still____ wa-ters.

VERSE
CHOIR (Unison)

3. He will re-fresh my soul: and guide me in right path-ways for his__ name's sake.

VERSE
T.B.
mf *cresc.*

4. Though I walk through the val - ley of the sha - dow of death I will fear no__ e - vil: for

Psalm 24: 1–5, 7

Music: Simon Mold

Moderato

RESPONSE

(**Rit.** and higher notes last time only.)

7. Lift up your heads O you gates_____ and the King of glo - ry shall come in.

Ped.

VERSE

SOLO OR CHOIR (Unison)

cresc.

Rx

1. The earth is the Lord's and all that is in it:_____ the com-pass of the world and those who dwell there-in.

Man.

VERSE

SOLO OR CHOIR (Unison)

dim. *cresc.*

Rx

2. For he has found-ed it up - on the seas:_____ and es-tab - lished it up - on the wa - ters.

Man.

VERSE

SOLO OR CHOIR (Unison)

ten.

Rx

3. Who shall as-cend the hill of the Lord:_____ or who shall stand in his ho - ly_ place?

Ped.

VERSE
CHOIR (Harmony, unaccompanied)

4. He that has clean hands and a pure heart: who has not set his soul up-on i-

- dols nor sworn his oath to a lie.

unis. *dim.* *ten.*

mp *dim.* *ten.*

Ped.

VERSE
CHOIR (Harmony)

meno f
and re-com-pense *cresc.* **rit.**

5. He shall re-ceive bless-ing from the Lord: and re - com-pense from the God of his sal - va - tion.

f Gt. *cresc.* Sw. *meno f* *cresc.* **rit.**

Man.

Ped.

Psalm 25: 3–6, 8

Music: Norman Warren

Psalm 26: 1–5, 8

Music: Peter White

RESPONSE

8. Lord I love the house of your ha - bi - ta - tion___ and the place where your glo - ry dwells.

VERSE

1. Give judgement for me O Lord   for I have walked in my   in - tegrity:
2. Put me to the test O   Lord   and   prove me:
3. For your steadfast love has been ever be -   fore   my   eyes:
4. I have not   sat   with de -   ceivers:
5. I hate the as -   sembly   of the   wicked:

℟

(1.) I have trusted in the Lord   and   not_____   wavered.
(2.) try my   mind_____   and   my   heart.
(3.) and   I   have   walked in   your   truth.
(4.) nor con -   sort - ed   with   the   hypocrites;
(5.) I will not   sit_____   with the   un -   godly.

Acc.

RESPONSE (after verse 5)

8. Lord I love the house of your ha - bi - ta - tion___ and the place where your glo - ry dwells.

PSALM 27: 1–5

Music: Simon Mold

Alla marcia

VERSE

3. If an ar-my en-camp a-gainst me_ my heart shall not_ be a-fraid:

Marcato e staccato

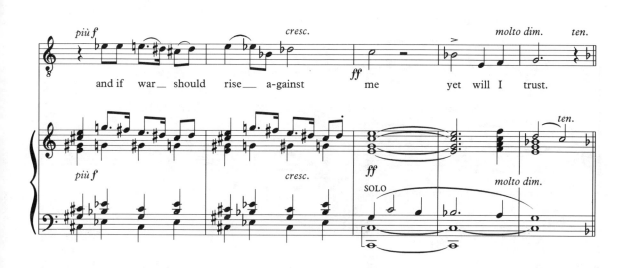

and if war_ should rise_ a-gainst me yet will I trust.

Andante

VERSE

CHOIR (Harmony, unaccompanied)

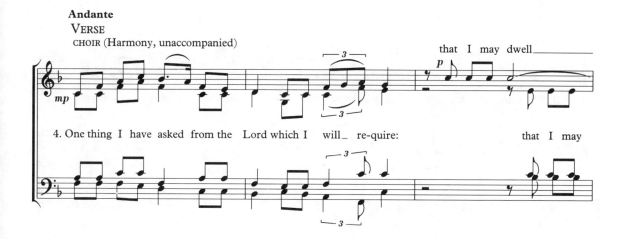

that I may dwell_____

4. One thing I have asked from the Lord which I will_ re-quire: that I may

_in the house of the Lord_____

dwell _in the house of the Lord all the days of my life,_

a tempo ma un poco meno mosso

5. to see the fair beau - ty of the Lord:_____ in his tem - ple.

and to seek his will in his tem - ple.

a tempo ma un poco meno mosso

pp ethereal

Ped.

RESPONSE (after verse 5)

1. The Lord is my light and my sal - va - tion: whom then shall___ I fear?

Ped.

PSALM 28: 1a, 7–10

Music: Michael Dawney

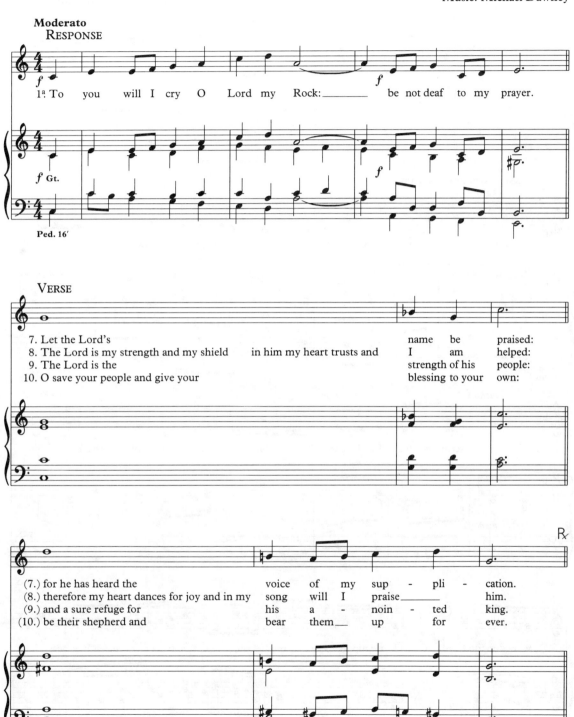

PSALM 29: 1–4, 9b

Music: Simon Mold

Psalm 30: 2–4, 11–12

Music: Norman Warren

Gently

RESPONSE

mf — *cresc.*

2. O Lord— my God I cried to you: and you— have made me whole.—

VERSE
SOLO OR CHOIR (Unison)

mp

3. You brought me back— O Lord from the land— of si - lence: you saved my

℞

life— from a-mong those that go down to the Pit.—

VERSE
SOLO OR CHOIR (Unison)

f

4. Sing prai-ses to the Lord all you his faith-ful ones: and give thanks to his ho - ly name.—

℞

Psalm 31: 1–5a

Music: Norman Warren

Psalm 32: 1, 9–12

Music: Norman Warren

Psalm 33: 1–5, 8

Music: Michael Dawney

Psalm 34: 1–4, 8–10

Music: Norman Warren

8. O taste and see that the Lord is good.

1. I will bless the Lord con-tin-ual-ly: his praise shall be al-ways in my mouth. 2. Let my

soul boast of the Lord: the hum-ble shall hear it and re-joice.

3. O praise the Lord with me: let us ex-alt his name to-ge-ther. 4. For I

sought the Lord's help and he ans - wered: and he freed_ me from all my fears._____

VERSE
CHOIR (Unison)   Harmony

mf
9. Fear the Lord all you his ho - ly ones, for those who fear him ne - ver lack. 10. Lions may

cresc.
suf - fer want and go hun - gry_ but those who fear the Lord lack_ no - thing good._____

RESPONSE (after verse 10)

mf
8. O taste and see that the Lord_____ is good,

DESCANT

f
O_ taste_ and_ see_ that the Lord_____ is_ good._____

f
O taste and see that the Lord_____ is good._____

Psalm 35: 1–4, 9a

Music: Noël Tredinnick

RESPONSE (Harmony)

9a Then shall my soul be joy-ful in the Lord,

joy - ful in the Lord, joy - ful in the Lord.

PSALM 36: 5–9

Music: Norman Warren

Psalm 37: 1–7a

Music: Norman Warren

VERSE
s.

4. Let the Lord_ be your de - light:_____ and he will grant you your heart's de - sire. Be

VERSE
CHOIR (Harmony)

5. Com-mit your way to the Lord:_____ trust him and he will act.___ Be

VERSE
CHOIR (Unison)

6. He will make your right-eous-ness shine as clear as the light: and your in-no-cence as the noon-day. Be

RESPONSE (after verse 6)

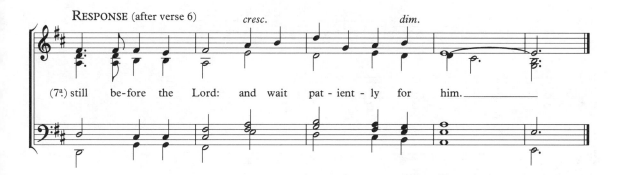

(7ª) still be-fore the Lord: and wait pat - ient - ly for him._____

Psalm 38: 15, 18–21

Music: David Iliff

VERSE

20. Those also who repay evil for good are a - gainst me:

(20.) because I seek_____ af - ter good.

21. Forsake me not O Lord go not far from me my God:

(21.) hasten to my help O Lord my sal - va - tion.

RESPONSE (after verse 21)

15. For in you Lord have I put my trust.

PSALM 39: 1, 4–8

Music: Simon Mold

* Omit rest before v.7, which begins on the 4th crotchet of the bar.

Psalm 40: 1–5

Music: Norman Warren

RESPONSE

3. The Lord has put a new song in my mouth:_____ a song of thanks-giv-ing to our

God._____

VERSE S.

1. I wait-ed pat-ient-ly for the Lord: and he in-clined to me and heard my cry.

VERSE T.B.

2. He brought me up from the pit of roar-ing wa-ters out of the mire and clay: and

set my feet up-on a rock and made firm___ my foot-hold.

Psalm 42: 1–7

Music: Peter White

night: while they ask me all day long 'Where now is your God?'

VERSE
T.B.

4. As I pour out my soul by my-self I re - mem - ber this:

how I went to the house of the Mighty One in - to the tem - ple of God.

VERSE
CHOIR (Unaccompanied)

dim.

5. To the shouts and songs of thanks - giv - ing: a mul - ti-tude keep-ing high fes - ti - val.

VERSE
T.B.

6. Why are you so full of hea - vi - ness my soul: and why so un-qui-et with - in me?

Psalm 43: 3–6a

Music: Response from *Tonus Peregrinus*
arranged Norman Warren
Verses Norman Warren

RESPONSE

6ª O put your trust in God:＿ for I will praise＿ him.

VERSE

3. O send out your light and your truth and let them lead me: let them guide me to your ho-ly

hill and to your＿ dwell-ing.

VERSE

T.B.

cresc. *cresc.*

mf

4. Then I shall go to the al - tar of God to God my joy and my de - light:__ and to the

harp__ I shall sing your__ prai - ses O God__ my_____ God.

dim.

℞

VERSE

CHOIR (Harmony)

mp

5. Why are you so full of hea - vi-ness my soul: and why so un-qui - et with - in me?

RESPONSE (after verse 5)

DESCANT

6ᵃ O put your trust in God:__ for__ I__ will praise_____ him.

f

6ᵃ O put your trust in God:__ for I will praise__ him.

Psalm 45: 1–4, 6a

Music: Barry Ferguson

VERSE

3. Gird your sword upon your thigh O migh - ty war - rior:

in glory and majesty tread down your foes and triumph!

VERSE

4. Ride on in the cause of truth:__ and for the sake of jus - tice.

RESPONSE (after verse 4)

DESCANT

6ª. Your throne is the throne of__ God: it en - dures____ for ev - er.

6ª. Your throne is the throne of__ God: it en - dures____ for ev - er.

Ped

Psalm 46: 1–3, 10–11

Music: Norman Warren

VERSE

CHOIR (Harmony)

cresc.

℞

3. Though the wa - ters rage and_ foam: and though the moun-tains quake at the ris-ing of the sea.

VERSE

T.B.

p

10. Be still and know that I am_ God: I will be ex-alt - ed a - mong the_ na - tions

cresc.

I will be ex - alt - ed up - on the_ earth.

RESPONSE (after verse 10)

f

11. The Lord of hosts is with us:___ the God of Ja - cob is our strong-hold.

PSALM 47: 1–7

Music: John Barnard

6. O sing prai - ses sing prai - ses to God:_ O sing prai - ses sing

prai - ses to_____ our King.

RESPONSE (after verse 6)
DESCANT (2nd time only)

7. God is the King_ of all the earth:_ O praise him in a

well - wrought psalm.

Psalm 50: 1–6

Music: Norman Warren

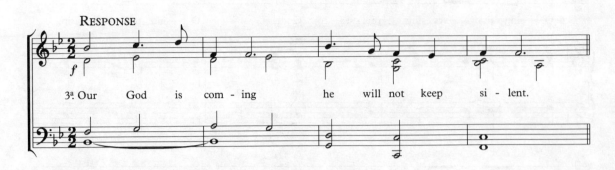

Response

3ª Our God is com-ing he will not keep si - lent.

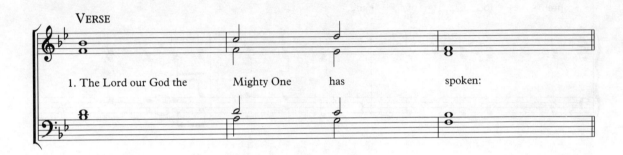

Verse

1. The Lord our God the Mighty One has spoken:

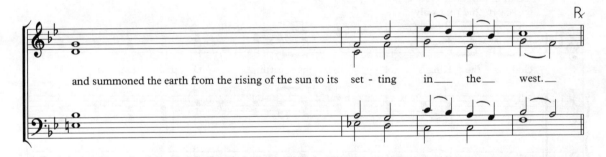

and summoned the earth from the rising of the sun to its set - ting in the west.

Verse

2. From Zion perfect in beauty: God has shone out in glo - ry.

4. He calls to the heavens a - bove: and to the earth so he may judge his __ peo - ple.

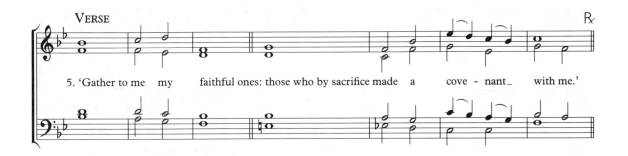

5. 'Gather to me my faithful ones: those who by sacrifice made a cove - nant __ with me.'

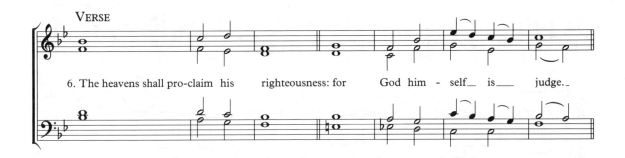

6. The heavens shall pro-claim his righteousness: for God him - self __ is __ judge. __

RESPONSE (after verse 6)

3ª Our God is com - ing he will not keep si - lent.

PSALM 51: 1–4, 10

Music: Simon Mold

3. For I ack-now-ledge my __ re-bel-lion: and __ my sin __ is ev-er be-fore me. Cre-

VERSE
CHOIR

4. A - gainst you on - ly have I sinned and done what is e - vil in __ your eyes:

so __ you will __ be just in your sen-tence and blame-less in __ your judg - ing. Cre -

RESPONSE (after verse 4)

-ate __ in me a clean heart O God: and re - new a right spi - rit with - in __ me.

Psalm 52: 1–4, 8–9

Music: David Iliff

VERSE
CHOIR (Harmony)

mf

3. You have loved evil and not good:— to tell lies ra-ther than to speak the truth.

4. You love all words that may do hurt:— and ev-ery de-ceit of the tongue.

℞

Lively
VERSE

9. I will al-ways give you thanks, for this was your do-ing:— I will

for this was your do-ing:_

glo-ri-fy your name be-fore the faith-ful for it is good— to praise you.

for it is good to praise you.

℞

PSALM 54: 1–4, 6

Music: Noel Rawsthorne

VERSE
S.A.   *cresc.*

4. But sure - ly God is my help - er: the Lord is the up-hold-er of my life.

VERSE
CHOIR (Unison)

6. Then will I of - fer you sac - ri-fice with a will - ing heart: I will praise your name O

Lord_____ for it is good.

RESPONSE (after verse 6)   *cresc.*

2. Hear my prayer O God: and lis - ten to the words of my mouth.

Psalm 56: 3, 8–12

Music: Norman Warren

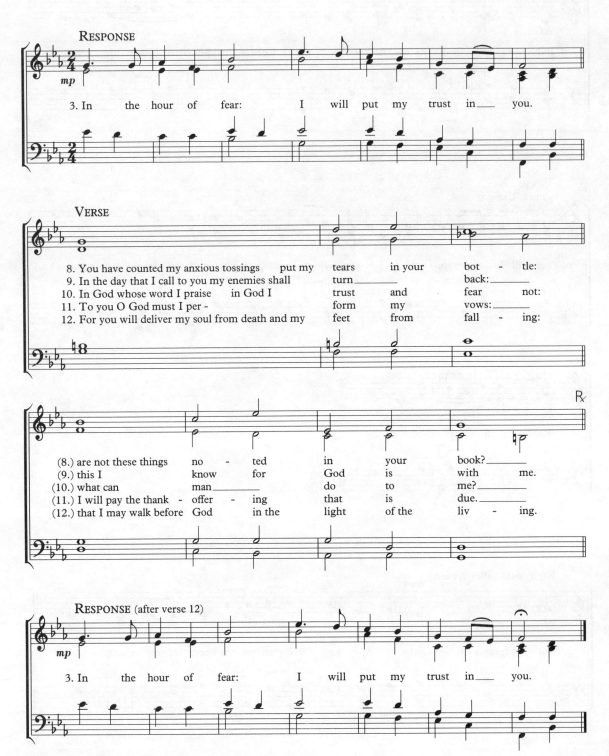

Psalm 57: 6, 8–11

Music: Norman Warren

Psalm 61: 2b–5, 8

Music: Norman Warren

PSALM 62: 1, 6–8

Music: Howard Stephens

Psalm 63: 1–5

Music: Norman Warren

VERSE

4. For your unchanging goodness is better than life:

(4.) there – fore my lips shall praise you.

℞

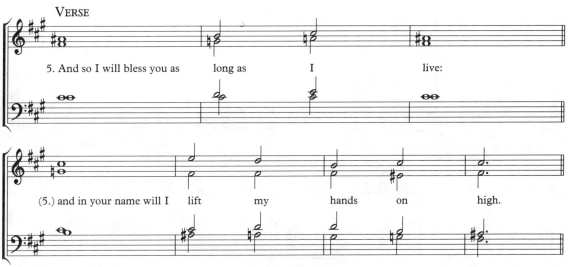

VERSE

5. And so I will bless you as long as I live:

(5.) and in your name will I lift my hands on high.

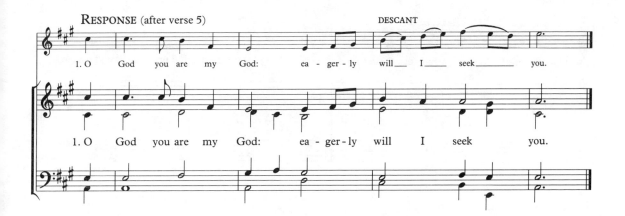

RESPONSE (after verse 5)   DESCANT

1. O God you are my God: ea - ger - ly will I seek you.

1. O God you are my God: ea - ger - ly will I seek you.

Psalm 65: 1, 8–13

Music: Norman Warren

VERSE
S.A.

10. You__ drench its fur-rows you le - vel the rid - ges be - tween: you

soft-en it with showers and bless its ear - ly growth.

VERSE
CHOIR (Harmony)
cresc.

11. You crown the year with your good-ness: and the tracks where you have passed drip with fat-ness.

VERSE
T.B.

12. The pas-tures of the wil-der-ness run____ o - ver: and the hills are gird-ed with joy.

VERSE
S.A.

cresc.

13. The mea-dows are clothed with sheep: and the val - leys stand so thick with corn they shout for joy and sing.

Psalm 67: 1–7

Music: Simon Mold

judge_____ the peo - ples with_ in - teg - ri - ty_____ and
God_____ our God_____ will bless_____ us,_____ and

R

gov - ern__ the na - tions up - on earth._____
God__ our__ God__ will__ bless us.

VERSE
CHOIR (Harmony, unaccompanied)

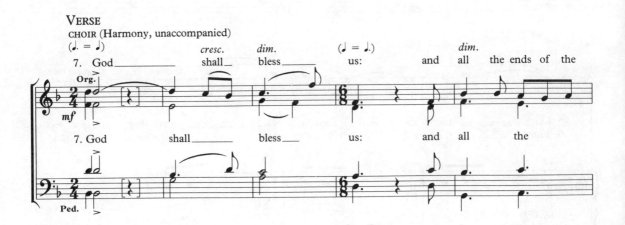

7. God_____ shall_ bless_____ us: and all the ends of the
7. God shall_____ bless__ us: and all the

earth___ will___ fear_____ him.

RESPONSE (after verse 7)

mf 1. Let God bless us: and

Con moto

mf 1. Let God_ be gra - cious to us_____ and bless us:

shine_____ up - on_____ us.

and make his face shine up - on_____ us.

Psalm 69: 32–38

Music: Noel Rawsthorne

Response

32. I will praise the name of God in a song: and glo-ri-fy him with thanks-giv - ing.

Verse

33. And that will please the Lord more than an ox:_____

(33.) more than a bull with horns and clo - ven hoof.

℞

34. Consider this you that are meek and re - joice:_ seek God and let your heart be glad.

Verse

35. For the Lord listens to the poor:_ he does not despise his ser - vants in cap - tivity.

36. Let the heavens and the earth___ praise him: the seas and all that moves in them.

VERSE

37. For God will save___ Zi - on: he will re - build the cities of Judah.

38. His people shall live there and possess it the seed of his servants shall in - herit it:

(38.) and those who love his name shall dwell in it.

RESPONSE (after verse 38)

32. I will praise the name of_ God in a song: and glo-ri-fy him with thanks-giv - ing.

PSALM 71: 19–23

Music: John Barnard

RESPONSE

19. Great are the things that you have done O God who is like you?

VERSE

20. You have burdened me with many and bitter troubles O turn and re - new me:

(20.) and raise me up a - gain from the depths of the earth.

21. Bless me beyond my for - mer great - ness:

(21.) O turn to me a - gain and comfort me.

VERSE

22. Then will I praise you upon the lute for your faithfulness O my God:

(22.) and sing your praises to the harp O Ho - ly One of Israel.

23. My lips shall re - joice in my sing - ing:

and my soul also for you have ransomed me.

RESPONSE (after verse 23)

mf

19. Great are the things that you have done O God who is like you?

Psalm 73: 24–26, 28

Music: Norman Warren

por - tion for ev - er.____

VERSE
CHOIR (Harmony)

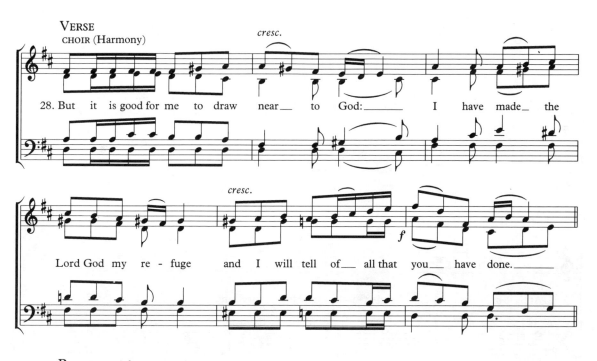

28. But it is good for me to draw near__ to God:_____ I have made__ the

Lord God my re - fuge and I will tell of__ all that you__ have done._____

RESPONSE (after verse 28)

24. You__ will guide__ me with__ your coun - sel: and af - ter-wards you__ will

lead me to glo - ry._____

Psalm 76: 1-4, 8-9, 11

Music: Norman Warren

Majestically

RESPONSE

4. Ra - diant in light are you: grea - ter in ma - jes-ty than the e-ter-nal hills.

VERSE

1. In Judah God is known: his name is great in Israel.

2. At Sa-lem is his___ taber-nacle: and his dwell-ing is___ in___ Zi - on.

VERSE

3. There he broke in pieces the flashing arrows of the bow:

(3.) the shield the sword and the weapons of battle.

8. You caused your sentence to be heard from _____ hea - ven:

(8.) the earth feared _____ and _____ was _____ still, _____

VERSE

9. when God a - rose to judgement: to save all the meek of the earth.

11. O make vows to the Lord your God and _____ keep them:

(11.) let all around him bring gifts to him that is wor - thy to _____ be _____ feared. _____

PSALM 77: 1, 7–8, 11–13

Music: Norman Warren

Gently

RESPONSE

1. I call to my God and sure-ly he will ans-wer me.

VERSE

T.B.

7. Will the Lord cast us off for ev - er: will he show us his fa-vour no more?

VERSE

S.A.

8. Is his mer-cy clean gone for ev - er: and his prom-ise come to an end for all ge-ne -

-ra - tions?

PSALM 80: 3b–5, 15, 18

Music: William Llewellyn

Strong and confident

RESPONSE

3b. Show us the light of your coun-te-nance___ and we shall be saved.

VERSE
CHOIR (Unison) OR SOLO

4. O Lord God of hosts: how long___ will you be an – gry at your

peo – ple's prayer?

VERSE

5. You have fed them with the bread of tears:_____ and

gi – ven them tears to drink in good mea – sure._____

Psalm 82: 1–4, 8

Music: Norman Warren

Brightly

RESPONSE

vv. 2, 4

8. A - rise O God and judge_____ the earth.

VERSE

s.

Rx

1. God has stood up in the coun - cil of heaven: in the midst of the gods he gives judge-ment.

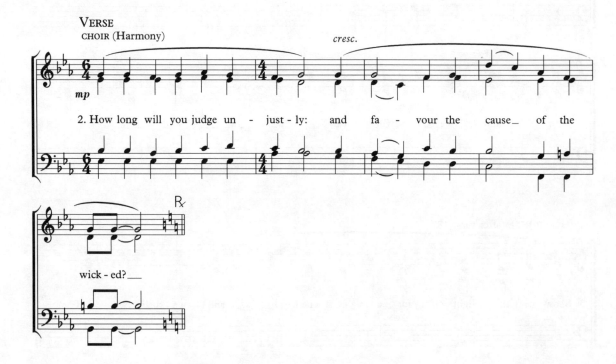

VERSE

CHOIR (Harmony)

cresc.

2. How long will you judge un - just - ly: and fa - vour the cause_ of the

Rx

wick - ed?___

VERSE
T.B.

cresc.

mf

3. Judge for the poor and fa-ther-less: vin-di-cate the af-flic-ted and op-pressed.

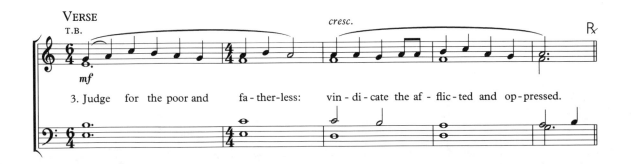

VERSE
CHOIR (Harmony)

cresc.

4. Res - cue the poor and nee - dy: and save them from the hands_ of the

wick - ed.___

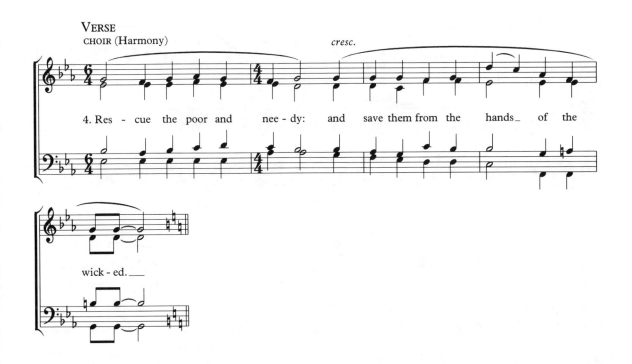

RESPONSE (after verse 4)

f

8. A - rise O God and judge_____ the earth.

PSALM 84: 1–4, 12

Music: David Wilson

VERSE

1. How love-ly is your dwell-ing-place: O Lord__ God of__ hosts!
2. How love-ly is your dwell-ing-place: O Lord__ God of__ hosts!

Man.

My soul has a de-sire and long - ing to__ en-ter the courts of the Lord:
My__ heart__ and my flesh re - joice in__ the liv - ing__ Lord.

Ped.

VERSE

3. The spar-row has found her a home and the swal - low a__ nest
4. E - ven your al - tar O Lord of hosts my_____ King__ and my_ God.

Man.

where she may lay her__ young: e - ven your al - tar O___ Lord.
Blessed are those who dwell in your house: they will__ al-ways be prais-ing you.

Ped.

PSALM 85: 1–2, 4–5, 7–9

Music: Noel Rawsthorne

RESPONSE

7ª. Show us your mer-cy O Lord, for I call to you all the day long.

VERSE

1. O Lord you were gracious to your land: you re-stored the__ fortunes of Jacob.

2. You forgave the iniquity of your people: and cov-ered all their_ sin.

VERSE

4. Return to us again O God our saviour: and let your_ an-ger cease from us.

5. Will you be displeased with us for ever:

(5.) will you stretch out your wrath from one gene - ra - tion to an - other?

VERSE

8. I will hear what the Lord God will speak:

(8.) for he will speak peace to his people to his faithful ones whose hearts are__ turned to him.

9. Truly his salvation is near to those that fear him: and his glory shall dwell in our land.

PSALM 89: 1–5

Music: William Llewellyn

3. The Lord said__ 'I have made____ a____

co - ve - nant with my cho - sen: I__ have sworn____ an

oath to my ser - vant Da - vid.'

VERSE

5. Let the heavens praise your won-ders O Lord:_____ and let your faith - ful-ness be sung in the as - sem - bly of the ho - ly ones.

cresc.

RESPONSE (after verse 5)

CHOIR

1ª. Lord I will sing for ev - er of your lov - ing kind-ness-es,_ kind-ness-es._____

Psalm 90: 1–4, 12

Music: Norman Warren

VERSE
S.
mf
cresc.

4. For a thou-sand years in your sight are like yes-ter-day pass-ing: or like_ one_

℞

watch of the night.

VERSE
CHOIR
f

12. Teach us so to num-ber our days:__ that we may ap-ply our hearts to wis-dom.

RESPONSE (after verse 12)
f
mp

1. Lord you have been our re-fuge: from one ge-ne-ra-tion to an-oth-er.

PSALM 91: 1–5, 9a

Music: Barry Ferguson

With confidence

RESPONSE

mf *f*

9ª. The Lord him-self is your re-fuge: the Most High is your strong-hold.

L'istesso tempo

VERSE legato

S.A. T.B.

mp

1. He who dwells in the shel-ter of the Most High:— who a - bides un - der the

Man. Ped.

CHOIR (Unison)

mp

sha - dow of the Al - migh - ty, 2. he will say to the Lord

'You are my re-fuge and my strong - hold: my God in whom I trust.' The

VERSE
T.B.

3. For he will de - li - ver you_____ from the snare_ of the hun - ter:

and from the de - stroy - ing curse. The

Psalm 92: 1–5

Music: David Iliff

VERSE

CHOIR (Unison)

3. Up - on the lute___ up - on the lute of ten strings: and to the

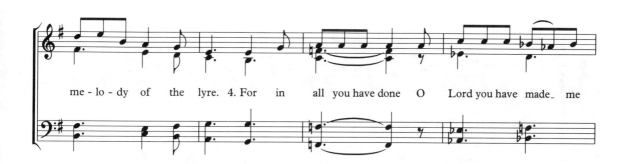

me - lo - dy of the lyre. 4. For in all you have done O Lord you have made_ me

glad:___ I will sing for joy be - cause of the works of your hands.

RESPONSE (after verse 4)

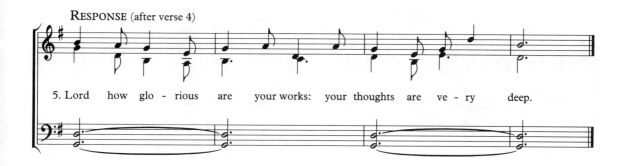

5. Lord how glo - rious are your works: your thoughts are ve - ry deep.

PSALM 95: 1–7

Music: Norman Warren

RESPONSE

1. Come let us sing out to the Lord: let us shout in tri-umph to the rock of our sal-va-tion.

VERSE
S.

2. Let us come be-fore his face with thanks-giv - ing: and cry out to him joy-ful-ly__ in__ psalms.

VERSE
T.B.

3. For the Lord is a great_____ God: and a great_____ king a-bove all gods.____

VERSE
S.

4. In__ his__ hand are the depths of the earth: and the peaks of the moun-tains are his.

VERSE
T.B.

5. The sea is his and he made it: his hands mould-ed dry land.

VERSE
CHOIR (Harmony)

6. Come let us wor-ship and bow down: and kneel be-fore the Lord our ma - ker.

VERSE
CHOIR (Harmony)

7. For he is the Lord our God: we are his peo-ple and the sheep of his pas - ture.

RESPONSE (after verse 7)

1. Come let us sing out to the Lord: let us shout in tri-umph to the rock of our sal-va-tion.

PSALM 97: 1–6

Music: Peter White

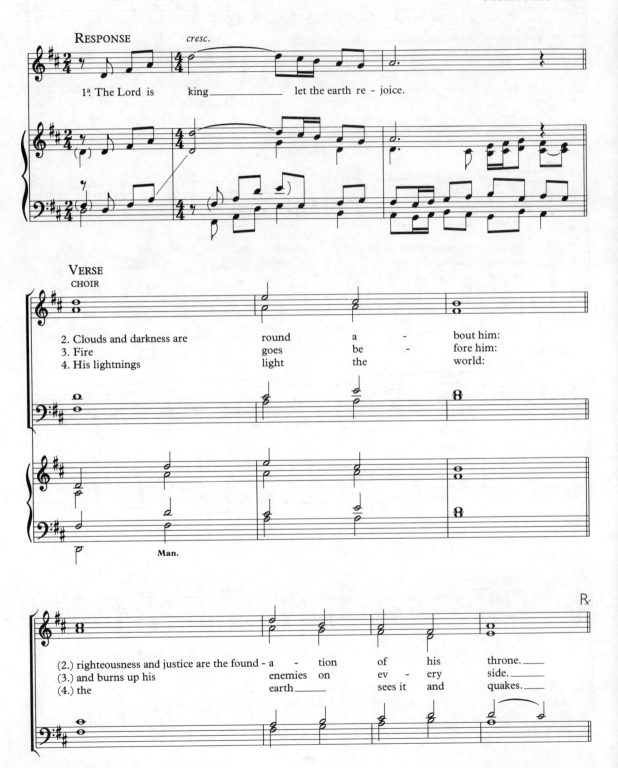

RESPONSE *cresc.*

1ª. The Lord is king_____ let the earth re - joice.

VERSE
CHOIR

2. Clouds and darkness are   round   a -   bout him:
3. Fire   goes   be -   fore him:
4. His lightnings   light   the   world:

Man.

(2.) righteousness and justice are the found - a - tion of   his   throne.____
(3.) and burns up his   enemies on ev - ery side.____
(4.) the   earth____ sees it and quakes.____

VERSE

CHOIR

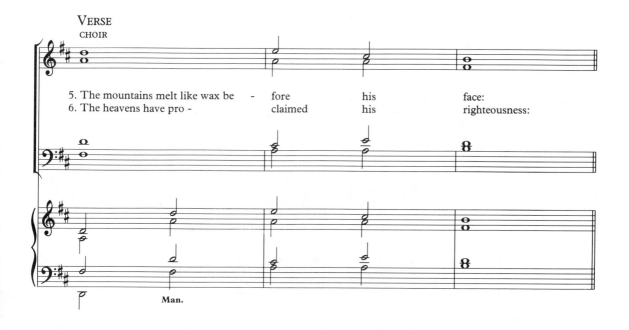

5. The mountains melt like wax be - fore his face:
6. The heavens have pro - claimed his righteousness:

Man.

R⁄

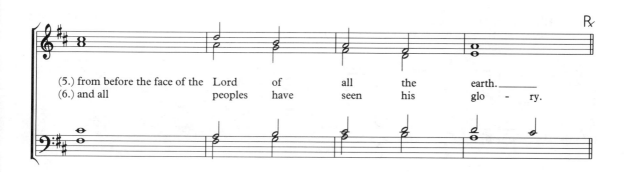

(5.) from before the face of the Lord of all the earth._____
(6.) and all peoples have seen his glo - ry.

RESPONSE (after verse 6)

cresc.

1ᵃ The Lord is king_____ let the earth re - joice.

PSALM 98: 1–6

Music: Simon Mold

*The verses may be sung by soloists, semichorus or full choir, as desired.

Dolce

(6.) up - on _____

Lord has made known his sal - va - tion: he has re - vealed his
all the ___ ends _____ of the earth have seen the sal - va - tion
me - lo - dy _____ to the Lord up - on the ___ harp: up -

___ the harp _____ with sounds _____ of ___ praise.

just de - li - ver - ance in the sight of the na - tions.
of our ___ God; have seen the sal - va - tion of ___ our ___ God.
- on the ___ harp and with the ___ sounds, the ___ sounds of ___ praise.

RESPONSE (after verse 6)

DESCANT

rit.

1ª O _____ sing ___ to the Lord a ___ new ___ song: sing ___ to the Lord all the earth.

_f_

1ª O sing to the Lord a new ___ song: sing to the Lord ___ all ___ the ___ earth.

rit.

Ped.

PSALM 100: 1, 2–4

Music: Norman Warren

Brightly

RESPONSE

1. O shout to the Lord in tri-umph all the earth: come be-fore his face with songs of joy.

VERSE
CHOIR (Harmony)

cresc.

2. Know that the Lord he is God: it is he who has made us and we__ are__ his__ we are his peo-ple and the sheep__ of his pas - ture.__

VERSE
CHOIR (Harmony)

3. Come in-to his gates with thanks - giv - ing____ and in - to his courts with__

Psalm 103: 1–5

Music: Norman Warren

RESPONSE

1ᵃ Praise the Lord O my soul: O my soul:

VERSE CHOIR (Harmony)

2. Praise the Lord O my soul:__ and for - get not all his be - ne - fits,_____

VERSE CHOIR (Harmony)

3. who for-gives all your sin: and heals_____ all your in - fir - mi - ties,___

VERSE CHOIR (Harmony)

4. who re-deems your_ life from the pit: and crowns you with mer - cy and com -

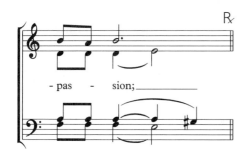

- pas - sion;_____

VERSE
CHOIR (Harmony)

5. who sa - tis-fies your be - ing with good___ things: so that your__ youth is re -

- newed like an ea - gle's.

RESPONSE (after verse 5)   DESCANT

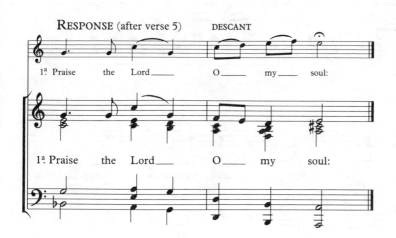

1ᵃ Praise the Lord____ O____ my___ soul:

1ᵃ Praise the Lord____ O____ my___ soul:

Psalm 104: 1, 4–6, 11, 13–14, 35

Music: Norman Warren

VERSE

CHOIR (Unison)

35. I will sing to the Lord as long as I___ live:

Harmony *cresc.*   **rall.** *cresc.*   **a tempo**

I will praise my God_____ while I___ have_ a - ny be - ing.

RESPONSE (after verse 35)

1. Praise the Lord my_ soul,   Praise the Lord O my soul:

O Lord God how great you are. Praise the Lord my_ soul.

Psalm 105: 1–5

Music: Simon Mold

Psalm 107: 1–3, 8–9

Music: William Llewellyn

VERSE

9. For he sat - is - fies___ the thir - sty: and
fills the hun - gry with good___ things.___

RESPONSE (after verse 9)

DESCANT

1. O give thanks to the Lord for he is good:___ for his lov - ing
1. O give thanks to the Lord for he is good: for his lov - ing

mer - cy is for ev - er.
mer - cy is___ for ev - er.

Psalm 108: 1–6

Music: Peter White

Verse

4. For the greatness of your mercy rea - ches to the heavens:_____ and your

faith - ful - ness to the clouds._____

Verse

5. Be exalted O God a-bove the heavens: and let your glory be

o - ver all the earth;_____

Verse

6. that those whom you love may be de - li - vered: O save us by your right hand and ans-wer me.

PSALM III: 1b–4

Music: Noel Rawsthorne

1b. I will praise the Lord with my whole heart, I will praise the Lord.

2. The works of the Lord are great: and stud-ied by all who take de-light in them.

3. His deeds are ma - jes - tic and glo - ri - ous: and his

right-eous-ness stands for ev - er.

VERSE
CHOIR (Unison)

4. His mar-vel-lous acts have won him a name to be re - mem - bered: the

Lord is gra - cious and mer - ci - ful.

RESPONSE (after verse 4)

1ᵇ I will praise the Lord with my whole heart, I will praise the Lord.

Psalm 112: 1, 4, 6–8

Music: Norman Warren

VERSE

S. cresc.

mf

7. He___ will not fear bad___ tid - ings: his heart____ is stead - fast___

℞

trust - ing in the Lord.

VERSE

T.B. cresc.

mf

8. His___ heart is con - fi - dent and will not fear: he will see the down - fall of___ his___

e - ne - mies.

RESPONSE (after verse 8) cresc.

mf

1ᵇ. Blessed are those who fear the Lord: and great-ly de-light in his___ com - mand-ments.___

PSALM 113: 1–6

Music: Simon Mold

in _____ hea - ven or up - on _____ the earth, (6.) who has his dwell - ing, his

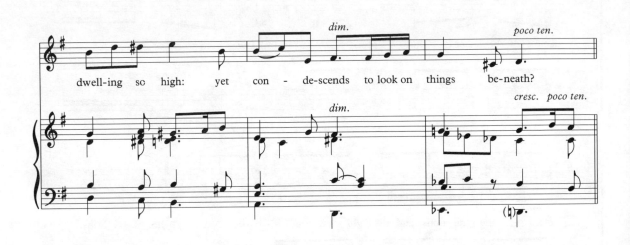

dwell-ing so high: yet con - de-scends to look on things be-neath?

RESPONSE (after verses 5 and 6)

2. Let the name of the Lord be blessed: from this time for - ward and for ev - er.

Ped.

Psalm 114: 1–8

PSALM 115: 1a, 12–15, 17

Music: Noel Rawsthorne

RESPONSE

1a. Not to us O Lord not to us but to your name give the glory.

VERSE
CHOIR (Harmony)

12. He will bless all those that fear the Lord: both high and low together.

VERSE
s.

13. May the Lord in - crease you great - ly: you and your child - ren af - ter you.

VERSE
T.B.

14. The bless - ing of the Lord be up - on you: he that made heaven and earth.

VERSE
s.

15. As for the heavens they are the Lord's: but the earth he has given to the child-ren of men.

VERSE
CHOIR (Unison)

17. But we will bless the__ Lord: both now_____ and for ev-er-more O praise the

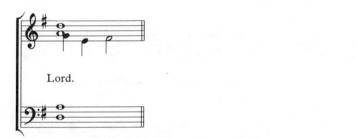

Lord.

RESPONSE (after verse 17)

1ª Not to__ us O Lord not to us but to your name give the__ glo - ry.

PSALM 116: 1, 3–6

Music: Simon Mold

PSALM 118: 1, 4–8

Music: Richard Lloyd

RESPONSE

1. O give thanks to the Lord for he— is good: his mer-cy en-dures for ev-er.—

VERSE
CHOIR (Harmony)

4. Let those who fear the Lord pro-claim: that his mer - cy en - dures___ for ev - er.

VERSE
s.

5. In my dan - ger I called to the Lord: he ans-wered and set— me— free.

VERSE
CHOIR (Harmony)

6. The Lord is on my side I shall not fear: what can

man do to me?

VERSE

T.B.

7. The Lord is at my side as my help - er: I shall see the
down-fall of my e - ne-mies.

VERSE

CHOIR (Harmony)   *cresc.*   *dim.*

8. It is bet - ter to take re - fuge in the Lord:_____ than to put your
trust in man.

RESPONSE (after verse 8)

1. O give thanks to the Lord for he__ is good: his mer-cy en-dures for ev-er.__

PSALM 119: 105–107, 111–112

Music: David Iliff

Music: © 1993 David Iliff / Jubilate Hymns

Psalm 119: 129–133, 135

Music: Norman Warren

Response

135. Make your face shine up-on your ser-vant: and teach me your stat-utes.

Verse

129. Wonderful are your com - mands:
130. The unfolding of your word gives light:
131. I open my mouth and draw in my breath:
132. O turn to me and be merci - ful to me:
133. Order my steps according to your word:

(129.) and therefore my soul keeps them.
(130.) it gives under - stand - ing to the sim - ple.
(131.) for I yearn for your command - ments.
(132.) as is your way with those who love your name.
(133.) that no evil may get master - y over me.

Response (after verse 133)

135. Make your face shine up-on your ser-vant: and teach me your stat-utes.

Psalm 121: 1–5, 7–8

Music: Norman Warren

Response

5. The Lord him-self is your keep-er: the Lord is your de - fence.

Verse

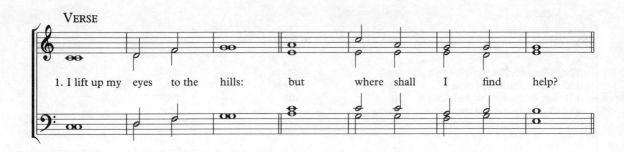

1. I lift up my eyes to the hills: but where shall I find help?

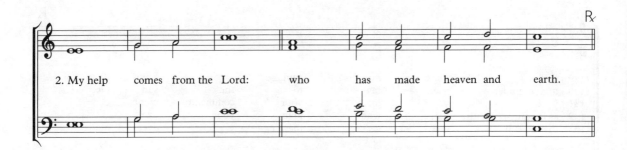

2. My help comes from the Lord: who has made heaven and earth.

Verse

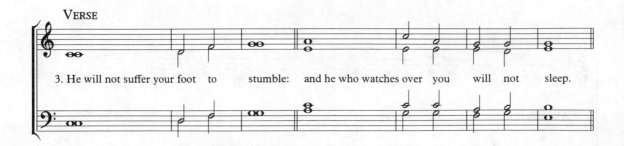

3. He will not suffer your foot to stumble: and he who watches over you will not sleep.

4. Be sure he who has charge of Israel: will nei - ther slumber nor sleep.

VERSE

7. The Lord will defend you from all___ evil: it is he who will guard your life.

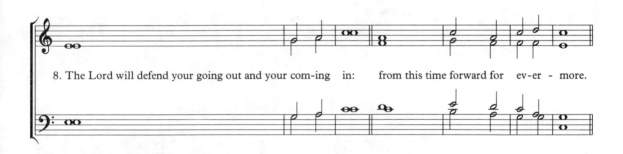

8. The Lord will defend your going out and your com-ing in: from this time forward for ev-er - more.

RESPONSE (after verse 8)

5. The Lord him-self is your keep-er: the Lord is your de - fence.

Psalm 122: 1, 6–9

Music: Norman Warren

Gently

RESPONSE

mf

1. I was glad when they said to me: 'Let us go to the house of the Lord.'

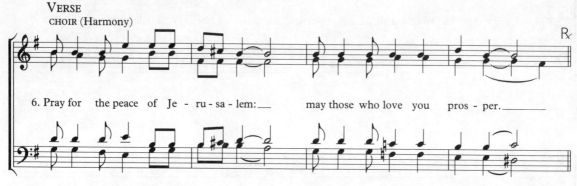

VERSE

CHOIR (Harmony)

6. Pray for the peace of Je - ru - sa - lem:___ may those who love you pros - per.___

VERSE   S.

mp

mf

(7.) Peace be with-in your walls: in___ your pa - la - ces.___

T.B.

mp

7. Peace be with-in your walls: and pros - pe - ri - ty in your pa - la - ces.___

VERSE
CHOIR (Harmony)

8. For the sake of my bro-thers and com - pan - ions:___ I will pray that peace be___

with you._____

VERSE
CHOIR (Harmony)

9. For the sake of the house of the Lord our God:___ I will seek for your

good._____

RESPONSE (after verse 9)
DESCANT

1. I was glad when they said to me: 'Let us go to the house of the Lord.'

mf

1. I was glad when they said to me: 'Let us go to the house of the Lord.'_____

Psalm 126: 1–7

Music: Norman Warren

Brightly

RESPONSE   *cresc.*   vv. 3, 4

6. Those that sow in tears: shall reap with songs of joy.

VERSE
T.B.   *cresc.*

1. When the Lord turned a-gain the for-tunes of Zi-on: then were we like men re - stored to life.

VERSE
S.   *cresc.*

2. Then was our mouth filled with laugh-ter: and our tongue with sing-ing.

VERSE
CHOIR (Harmony)

3. Then said they a-mong the hea-then: 'The Lord has done great things for them.'

PSALM 127: 1–6

Music: Barry Ferguson

Psalm 130: 1–7

Music: Verses from Purcell
J. Turle
Response Norman Warren

RESPONSE

7. Trust in the Lord: for with him there is mer-cy.

VERSE

1. Out of the depths have I called to you O Lord: Lord hear my voice;

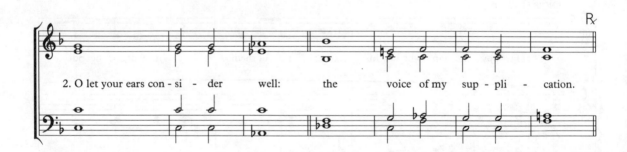

2. O let your ears con-si-der well: the voice of my sup-pli-cation.

VERSE

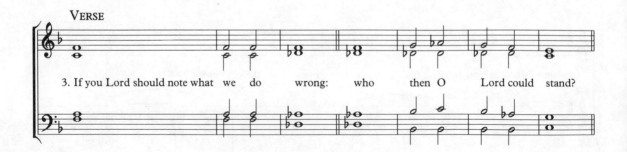

3. If you Lord should note what we do wrong: who then O Lord could stand?

Psalm 131: 1–4

Music: Richard Lloyd

RESPONSE

cresc. *mf* *dim.* vv. 2, 3

4. Trust in the Lord: from this time for-ward and for ev - er.

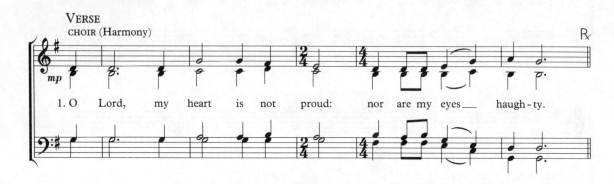

VERSE
CHOIR (Harmony)

mp

1. O Lord, my heart is not proud: nor are my eyes__ haugh-ty.

VERSE
CHOIR (Harmony)

mp *cresc.*

2. I do not bu-sy__ my-self in great mat-ters: or in things__ too

dim.

won - der-ful for me.

VERSE

S. OR SOLO

3. But I have calmed and qui-et-ed my soul like a weaned_____

child up-on its mo — ther's breast: like a child on its mo — ther's

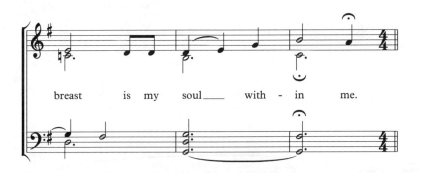

breast is my soul_____ with - in me.

RESPONSE (after verse 3)

4. Trust in the Lord: from this time for-ward and for ev - er.

PSALM 133: 1–4

Music: Norman Warren

RESPONSE

1. How good and love - ly it is: when we live to-geth-er in u – ni - ty.

VERSE

S.

2. It is fra - grant as oil up-on the head that runs＿ down o-ver the beard: fra-grant as

oil up-on the beard of＿ Aa-ron that ran＿ down o-ver the col - lar of his robe.＿

VERSE

CHOIR (Harmony) *cresc.*

dim.

℞

mf

3. It is like a dew of Her-mon: like the dew that falls up - on the hill__ of__ Zi - on.__

VERSE

CHOIR (Unison)

cresc.

℞

f

4. For there the_ Lord has com - mand-ed his bless-ing: which is life for ev - er - more._____

RESPONSE (after verse 4)

mf

1. How good and love - ly it is: when we live to-geth-er in u - ni-ty.

Psalm 135: 1b–3, 5–6

Music: Norman Warren

RESPONSE

1b Praise the name of the Lord: praise him you ser - vants of the Lord.

VERSE

2. Who stand in the house of the Lord: in the courts of the house of our God.

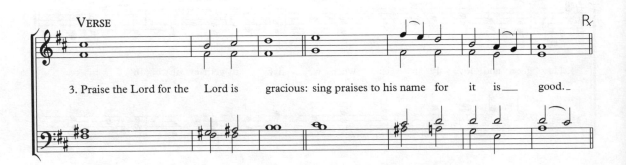

VERSE

3. Praise the Lord for the Lord is gracious: sing praises to his name for it is good.

VERSE

5. I know that the Lord is great: and that our Lord is a - bove all gods.

VERSE

6. He does whatever he wills in heaven and up - on the earth:

in the seas and in the great depths.

RESPONSE (after verse 6)

1℣. Praise the name of the Lord: praise him you ser - vants of the Lord.

Psalm 139: 1–5, 23a

Music: Howard Stephens

Response

mf

23ª Search me out O___ God and know my___ heart.

Verse
choir (Unison)

mf

1. O Lord you have searched me out and known me: you know when I sit or when I stand you com - pre-hend my thoughts long be - fore.

℞

Verse
choir (Harmony)

mf

2. You dis-cern my path___ and the pla - ces where I___ rest:___ you are ac - quaint - ed with all my___ ways.

℞

PSALM 140: 1–7

Music: Richard Lloyd

Psalm 142: 1–6

Music: Norman Warren

RESPONSE

6ᵇ I__ call to you O Lord   I say 'You are my re-fuge'.

VERSE

1. I call to the Lord with a loud__ voice:_ with loud voice I en-treat his__ fa-vour.

VERSE

2. I pour out my com-plaint be – fore him: and tell him__ all__ my__ trou-ble.

VERSE

3. When my spirit is faint within me you know my path:_____

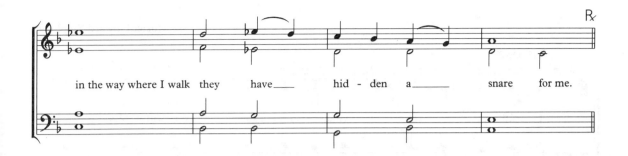

in the way where I walk they have__ hid - den a__ snare for me.

VERSE

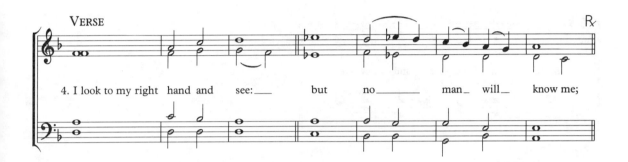

4. I look to my right hand and see:__ but no__ man_ will_ know me;

VERSE

5. all es - cape is gone:__ and there is no one who cares_ for__ me.__

RESPONSE (after verse 5)

6ᵇ. I__ call to you O Lord I say 'You are my re-fuge'.

Psalm 145: 1–5

Music: Howard Stephens

great - ness is past____ search - ing____ out.

VERSE
CHOIR (Harmony)

4. One generation shall praise your works____ to an - oth - er:

and de - clare____ your migh - ty____ acts.

VERSE
CHOIR (Harmony)

5. As for me I will be talking of the glorious splen - dour of your ma - jes - ty:

I will tell the sto - ry of____ your mar - vel - lous____ works.

Psalm 146: 1–3, 5–7

Music: Norman Warren

whose hope is in the Lord his God,

VERSE

S.

mf *cresc.*

6. the God who made hea-ven and_ earth:__ the sea____ and all that is in them, 7. who

T.B.

f

keeps_ faith for ev - er: who deals jus - tice to those that are opp - ressed.

RESPONSE (after verse 7)

DESCANT

f 1. Praise the_ Lord O my soul: while I live I will praise the_ Lord.

cresc.

f

1. Praise the Lord O my soul: while I live I will praise the Lord.

Psalm 147: 1, 3–7

Music: Norman Warren

Majestically

RESPONSE

vv. 3–4, 6

5ᵃ Great is our Lord and great___ is his power:

VERSE
CHOIR (Unison)

1. O praise the Lord. For it is good to sing prai-ses to our God: and to praise him is joy-ful__ and right.

VERSE
CHOIR (Harmony)

3. He heals the bro-ken in spi-rit: and binds up their wounds. 4. He counts the num-ber of the stars: and calls them all by name.___

6. The Lord re - stores____ the hum - ble: but he brings down the

wick - ed to the dust. ____

7. O sing to the Lord__ a song of thanks-giv-ing: sing prai-ses to our God__ up - on ____ the harp.

RESPONSE

5ª Great is our Lord and great____ is his power.

Psalm 148: 1–5

Music: Response traditional French
arranged Norman Warren
Verses Norman Warren

Response

1ᵃ Praise the Lord from hea - ven: praise him— in the heights.

Verse

s.

cresc.

℞

2. Praise him all his an - gels: O praise him— all— his— host.

Verse

s.

cresc.

℞

3. Praise him sun and moon:——— praise him— all you stars of light.

VERSE
T.B.

4. Praise him you high - est hea - ven:___ and you wa-ters that_ are a-bove the hea-vens.

VERSE
CHOIR (Unison)

5. Let them praise the name of the Lord:_____ for he com - man - ded and they were made.

RESPONSE (after verse 5)

1ª Praise the Lord from hea - ven: praise him_ in the heights.

Psalm 149: 1a, 3–6

Music: Norman Warren

Psalm 150: 1–6a

Music: John Barnard

VERSE
CHOIR

3. Praise him in the blast of the ram's horn: praise him on the lute__ and harp.

4. Praise him with the tim-brel and dan-ces: praise him on the strings and pipe._____

RESPONSE
ALL

Let ev-ery-thing that__ has breath praise__ the Lord:

MAGNIFICAT

Music: Norman Warren

VERSE

CHOIR (Unison)

8. He has come to the help of his ser-vant Is-ra-el:__ for he has re-mem-bered his

pro__ mise of me__ rcy,__9. the pro-mise he made to our fa__ thers: to

poco rall.

A - bra - ham__ and his child-ren for - ev - er.

RESPONSE (after verse 9)

cresc. *dim.*

3. The Al - migh-ty has done great things for__ me: and ho - ly is his__ name.

Nunc Dimittis

Music: Norman Warren

RESPONSE

Glo-ry to the Fa - ther and to the Son: and to the Ho - ly Spi - rit:

VERSE
T.B.

1. Lord now you let your ser - vant go in peace: your word has been ful - filled.

VERSE
T.B.

2. My own eyes have seen the sal - va - tion: which you have pre - pared in the

sight of ev - ery peo - ple;

poco meno mosso

VERSE

S.

f 3. a light___ to___ the___ na - tions:___ and the *cresc.*

T.B.

3. a light___ to re - veal you to the na - tions:___ and the *cresc.*

glo - ry of your peo - ple Is - ra - el.

glo - ry of your peo - ple Is - ra - el.

RESPONSE (after verse 3)

mf

Glo - ry to the Fa - ther and to the Son: and to the Ho - ly Spi - rit:

A - men.

The Easter Anthems

Music: Norman Warren

In memory of Michael Skinner 16.3.92

Te Deum I

Music: Norman Warren

RESPONSE

4. Ho - ly ho - ly ho - ly Lord God___ of pow - er and might: heaven and earth are full of your glo - ry. Ho - ly ho - ly Lord.

VERSE
CHOIR (Harmony)

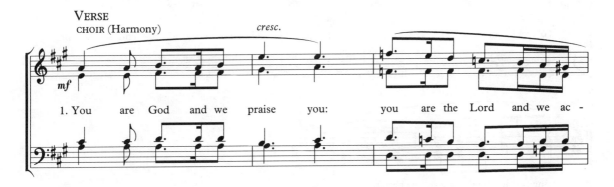

1. You are God and we praise you: you are the Lord and we ac -

- claim___ you;___

TE DEUM II

Music: Norman Warren

be_____ our judge.

VERSE
CHOIR (Unison)

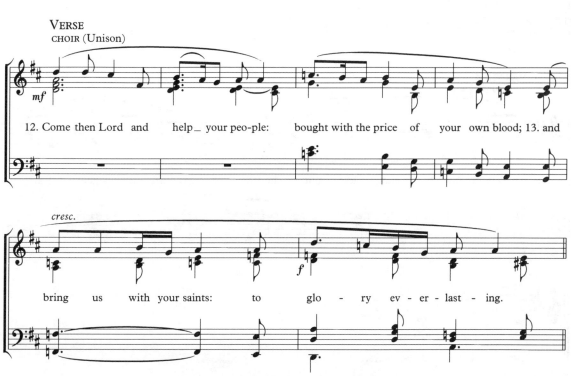

12. Come then Lord and help_ your peo-ple: bought with the price of your own blood; 13. and

cresc.

bring us with your saints: to glo - ry ev - er - last - ing.

RESPONSE (after verse 12)   DESCANT

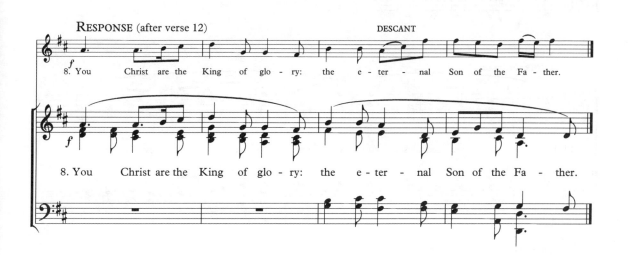

8. You Christ are the King of glo - ry: the e - ter - nal Son of the Fa - ther.

8. You Christ are the King of glo - ry: the e - ter - nal Son of the Fa - ther.

Te Deum III

Music: Norman Warren

VERSE
UNISON OR T.B.

16. Keep us to-day___ Lord___ from all sin:___ have mer - cy___ on___ us___

℞

Lord___ have___ mer - cy.

VERSE
CHOIR (Harmony)

18. In you Lord is our hope: let us not be con-found-ed at the last.___

RESPONSE (after verse 18)

17. Lord show us your love and mer - cy: for we___ put our trust in you.

GLORIA IN EXCELSIS

Music: Norman Warren

BLESS THE LORD

Music: Norman Warren

Saviour of the World

Music: Norman Warren

peo - ple.____

VERSE

S.

mf

5. Make your-self known as our sav - iour and migh - ty de - liv - er - er:　save us and help_ us that

cresc.

we___ may_ praise you._

VERSE

CHOIR (Harmony)　*cresc.*

mp

6. Come now and dwell with us___ Lord_ Je - sus Christ:_____ hear our prayer

dim.

and be with us al - ways.___

VERSE
CHOIR (Harmony)

Maestoso

cresc.

mf

7. And when you come_ in your_ glo - ry: make us to be one with you: and to

f

ff

cresc.

cresc.

share_ the life, the_ life_ of your king - dom, your king - dom.

to share_ the life_ of your king - dom, your king - dom._

RESPONSE (after verse 7)

DESCANT

1. Je - sus sav - iour of_ the_ world come to_ us_ in_ your_ mer - cy.

1. Je - sus sav - iour of_ the world come to_ us_ in_ your_ mer - cy.

OUR FATHER

Music: Norman Warren

RESPONSES

PSALM 1: 1–4, 7a

7ª For the Lord cares for the way __ of the right - eous. ___

PSALM 3: 1–5

3ª You Lord are a - bout me as a shield. _____

PSALM 7: 7–11

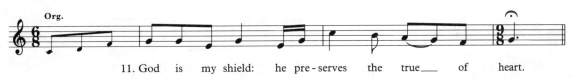

11. God is my shield: he pre - serves the true __ of heart.

PSALM 8: 1, 4–7

1. O Lord our Gov-er-nor: how glo - rious is your name in all the earth.

Psalm 9: 1, 8–11

1. I will give you thanks O___ Lord with my whole___ heart.

Psalm 10: 13–18a

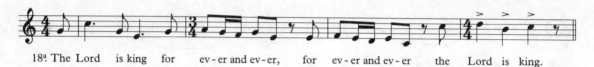

18ª. The Lord is king for ev - er and ev - er, for ev - er and ev - er the Lord is king.

Psalm 11: 1–4, 7

4. The Lord is in his ho - ly place the Lord is en - throned in heaven.___

Psalm 15: 1–7

7. They that do___ these_ things: shall ne - ver be o - ver - thrown.

PSALM 16: 1, 5–8

1. Pre-serve me O God: in you have I ta-ken re-fuge.__

PSALM 17: 4–8

7ª Show me the won-ders of your stead-fast love.

PSALM 18: 1, 32–34

1. I love_ you_ O__ Lord my strength: my__ for-tress and my de-liv-er-er.

PSALM 19: 1–6

1. The hea-vens de-clare the glo-ry of God, and the fir-ma-ment pro-claims his han-di-work.

Psalm 19: 7–10, 14b

14b. The Lord is my strength and my re - deem - er.

Psalm 20: 1–4, 7b

7b. We will trust in the name of the Lord our God.

Psalm 22: 23–26, 29

29. For the king-dom is the Lord's: and he shall be ru - ler o - ver the na - tions.

Psalm 23: 1–4, 6

1. The Lord is my shep-herd: there-fore can I lack no-thing, there-fore can I lack no-thing.

Response (last time)

1. The Lord is my shep-herd: there-fore can I lack no-thing, there-fore can I lack no-thing.

Psalm 24: 1–5, 7

7. Lift up your heads O you gates____ and the King of glo - ry shall come in.

Psalm 25: 3–6, 8

3. Show me your ways O Lord: and teach__ me your paths.

Psalm 26: 1–5, 8

8. Lord I love the house of your ha - bi - ta - tion____ and the place where your glo - ry dwells.

Psalm 27: 1–5

1. The Lord is my light and my sal - va - tion:_ whom then shall__ I fear?

PSALM 28: 1a, 7–10

1ᵃ. To you will I cry O Lord my Rock:_____ be not deaf to my prayer.

PSALM 29: 1–4, 9b

9ᵇ. The Lord sits_ en - throned as a king_ for ev - er.

PSALM 30: 2–4, 11–12

2. O Lord_ my God I cried to you: and you_ have made_ me whole._

PSALM 31: 1–5a

5ᵃ. In - to your hands I com - mit my_____ spi - rit.

PSALM 32: 1, 9–12

1. Bless-èd is he___ whose sin is for-given: whose i - ni - qui - ty is put___ a-way.

PSALM 33: 1–5, 8

8. Let the whole earth fear the Lord:___ and stand in awe of him.___

PSALM 34: 1–4, 8–10

8. O taste and see that the Lord___ is good.

PSALM 35: 1–4, 9a

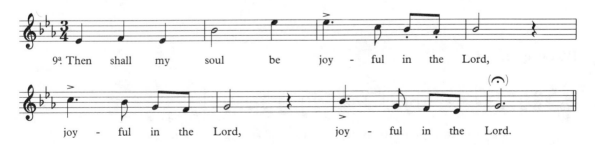

9a. Then shall my soul be joy - ful in the Lord,

joy - ful in the Lord, joy - ful in the Lord.

PSALM 36: 5–9

9. For with you is the well_ of__ life_____ and in your light shall we_ see_ light.

PSALM 37: 1–7a

7a Be still be-fore the Lord: and wait pat-ient-ly for him.

PSALM 38: 15, 18–21

15. For in you Lord have I put my trust.

PSALM 39: 1, 4–8

1. I will keep watch o-ver my ways I will keep a guard on my_ mouth.

Psalm 40: 1–5

3. The Lord has put a new song in my mouth:__ a song of thanks-giv-ing to our God.__

Psalm 42: 1–7

7. O put__ your trust__ in God:_____ for I will praise him, for

I will praise him my de - liv - er - er and__ my God._____

Psalm 43: 3–6a

6a O put your trust in God:__ for I will praise__ him.

Psalm 45: 1–4, 6a

6a Your throne is the throne of__ God: it en - dures_____ for ev - er.

PSALM 46: 1–3, 10–11

11. The Lord of hosts is with us:____ the God of Ja-cob is our strong-hold.

PSALM 47: 1–7

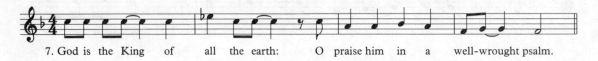

7. God is the King of all the earth: O praise him in a well-wrought psalm.

PSALM 50: 1–6

3ᵃ Our God is com - ing he will not keep si - lent.

PSALM 51: 1–4, 10

10. Cre - ate__ in me a clean heart O God: and re - new a right spi - rit with - in____ me.____

Psalm 52: 1–4, 8–9

8ᵇ I will trust in the good-ness of God for ev-er and ev - er.

Psalm 54: 1–4, 6

2. Hear my prayer O God: and lis-ten to the words of my mouth.

Psalm 56: 3, 8–12

3. In the hour of fear: I will put my trust in____ you.

Psalm 57: 6, 8–11

6. Let your__ glo-ry be o-ver all the earth.

PSALM 61: 2b–5, 8

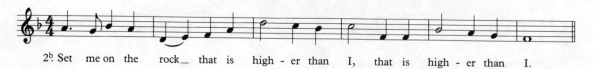

2b. Set me on the rock__ that is high-er than I, that is high-er than I.

PSALM 62: 1, 6–8

1. My soul waits in sil-ence for God:_____ for from him comes

my_____ sal-va-tion.

PSALM 63: 1–5

1. O God you are my God: ea-ger-ly will I seek you.

PSALM 65: 1, 8–13

1. You are to be praised O God: you that ans-wer prayer.

PSALM 67: 1–7

1. Let God be gra-cious to us and bless us:
and make his face shine up-on us.

PSALM 69: 32–38

32. I will praise the name of God in a song: and glo-ri-fy him with thanks-giv-ing.

PSALM 71: 19–23

19. Great are the things that you have done O God who is like you?

PSALM 73: 24–26, 28

24. You will guide me with your coun-sel: and af-ter-wards you will lead me to glo-ry.

Psalm 76: 1–4, 8–9, 11

4. Ra - diant in light are you: great - er in ma - jes - ty than the e - ter - nal hills.

Psalm 77: 1, 7–8, 11–13

1. I call___ to my God and sure - ly he will___ ans - wer me.

Psalm 80: 3b–5, 15, 18

3b Show us the light of your coun - te - nance___ and we shall be saved.

Psalm 82: 1–4, 8

8. A - rise O God and judge_____ the earth.

PSALM 84: 1–4, 12

12. O Lord God of hosts: bless-èd is the man who puts his trust in you. O Lord God of hosts: bless-èd is the man who puts his trust in you. O Lord of hosts, my King and my God.

Music: © 1993 David Wilson / Jubilate Hymns

PSALM 85: 1–2, 4–5, 7–9

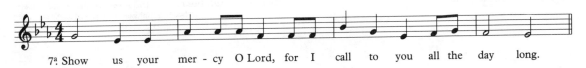

7ᵃ Show us your mer-cy O Lord, for I call to you all the day long.

Music: © 1993 Noel Rawsthorne

PSALM 89: 1–5

1ᵃ Lord I will sing for ev - er of your lov - ing kind - ness - es.

Music: © 1993 William Llewellyn
Reprinted by permission of Oxford University Press

PSALM 90: 1–4, 12

1. Lord you have been our re - fuge: from one ge - ne - ra - tion to an - oth - er.

Music: © 1993 Norman Warren / Jubilate Hymns

Psalm 91: 1–5, 9a

9ª. The Lord him-self is your re-fuge: the Most High— is your strong-hold.

Psalm 92: 1–5

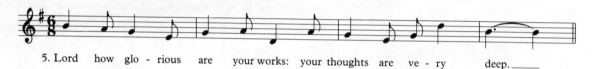

5. Lord how glo - rious are your works: your thoughts are ve - ry deep._____

Psalm 95: 1–7

1. Come let us sing out to the Lord: let us shout in tri-umph to the rock of our sal-va - tion.

Psalm 97: 1–6

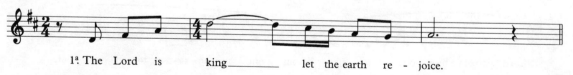

1ª. The Lord is king_____ let the earth re - joice.

PSALM 98: 1–6

1ᵃ O sing to the Lord a new song: sing to the Lord all the earth.

PSALM 100: 1, 2–4

1. O shout to the Lord in tri-umph all the earth: come be-fore his face with songs of joy.

PSALM 103: 1–5

1ᵃ Praise the Lord O my soul.

PSALM 104: 1, 4–6, 11, 13–14, 35

1. Praise the Lord my soul, Praise the Lord O my soul:

O Lord God how great you are. Praise the Lord my soul.

PSALM 105: 1–5

1ᵃ O ___ give thanks ___ to the Lord and call up - on his name.

PSALM 107: 1–3, 8–9

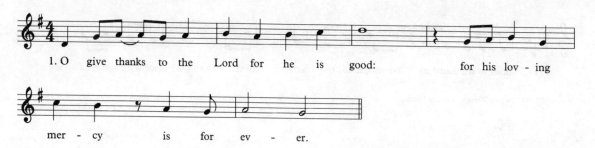

1. O give thanks to the Lord for he is good: for his lov - ing

mer - cy is for ev - er.

PSALM 108: 1–6

1. O God my heart ___ is fixed: ___ I will sing and make me - lo - dy. ___

PSALM 111: 1b–4

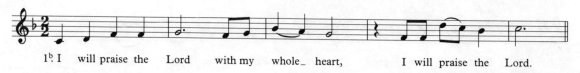

1ᵇ I will praise the Lord with my whole ___ heart, I will praise the Lord.

PSALM 112: 1, 4, 6–8

1b Blessed are those who fear the Lord: and great-ly de-light in his___ com-mand-ments.

Music: © 1993 Norman Warren / Jubilate Hymns

PSALM 113: 1–6

2. Let the name of the Lord be blessed: from this time for-ward and___ for ev — er.

Music: © Simon Mold

PSALM 114: 1–8

7a Trem-ble, trem-ble O earth___ at the pre-sence of the Lord:_____

Music: © 1993 Barry Ferguson

PSALM 115: 1a, 12–15, 17

1a Not to___ us O Lord not to us but to your name give___ the___ glo-ry.

Music: © 1993 Noel Rawsthorne

Psalm 116: 1, 3–6

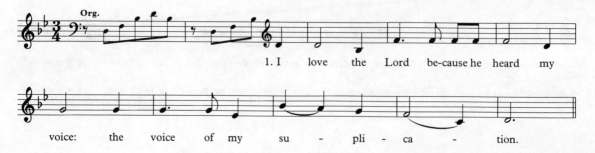

1. I love the Lord be-cause he heard my voice: the voice of my sup - pli - ca - tion.

Music: © 1993 Simon Mold

Psalm 118: 1, 4–8

1. O give thanks to the Lord for he__ is good: his mer-cy en-dures for ev-er.__

Music: © 1993 Richard Lloyd

Psalm 119: 105–107, 111–112

105. Your word is a lan - tern to my feet: and a light to my path.

Music: © 1993 David Iliff / Jubilate Hymns

Psalm 119: 129–133, 135

135. Make your face shine up - on your ser - vant: and teach__ me your stat - utes.

Music: © 1993 Norman Warren / Jubilate Hymns

PSALM 121: 1–5, 7–8

5. The Lord him-self is your keep-er: the Lord is your de - fence.

PSALM 122: 1, 6–9

1. I was glad when they said to me: 'Let us go to the house of the Lord.'

PSALM 126: 1–7

6. Those that sow in_ tears: shall_ reap with songs of_ joy.

PSALM 127: 1–6

1. Un - less the Lord build the house: their la-bour is but lost that build it.

Psalm 130: 1–7

7. Trust in the Lord: for with him there is mer - cy.

Psalm 131: 1–4

4. Trust in the Lord: from this time for-ward and for ev - er.

Psalm 133: 1–4

1. How good and love - ly it is: when we live to-geth-er in u - ni - ty.

Psalm 135: 1b–3, 5–6

1b. Praise the name of the Lord: praise him you ser - vants of the Lord.

PSALM 139: 1–5, 23a

23ᵃ Search me out O___ God and know my___ heart.

PSALM 140: 1–7

7. O Lord my God, you are my sure___ strong-hold.

PSALM 142: 1–6

6ᵇ I___ call to you O Lord I say 'You are my re-fuge'.

PSALM 145: 1–5

1. I will ex-alt you O God___ my king: I will bless___ your
name for ev-er and ev-er.

PSALM 146: 1–3, 5–7

1. Praise the Lord O my soul: while I live I will praise the Lord.

PSALM 147: 1, 3–7

5ᵃ Great is our Lord and great is his power.

PSALM 148: 1–5

1ᵃ Praise the Lord from hea - ven: praise him in the heights.

PSALM 149: 1a, 3–6

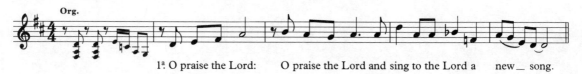

1ᵃ O praise the Lord: O praise the Lord and sing to the Lord a new song.

Psalm 150: 1–6a

6ª Let ev - ery-thing that___ has breath___ praise___ the Lord!

Magnificat

3. The Al - migh - ty has done great things for___ me: and ho - ly is his___ name.

Nunc Dimittis

Glo - ry to the Fa - ther and to the Son: and to the Ho - ly Spi - rit:

The Easter Anthems

Christ is ri - sen from the dead: glo - rious day we ce - le - brate.

Te Deum I

4. Ho - ly ho - ly ho - ly Lord God__ of pow - er and might:

heaven and earth are full of your glo - ry. Ho - ly ho - ly Lord.

Te Deum II

8. You Christ are the King of glo - ry: the e - ter - nal Son of the Fa - ther.

Te Deum III

17. Lord show us your love and mer - cy: for we__ put our trust in you.

Gloria in Excelsis

1. Glo - ry__ to God,__ glo - ry to God in the high - est:__

glo - ry__ to God__ and peace to his peo-ple on earth.

Bless the Lord

Bless the Fa - ther the Son and Ho-ly Spi - rit: sing his praise and ex - alt him for ev - er.

Saviour of the World

1. Je - sus sav - iour of__ the world come to__ us___ in__ your mer - cy.

Our Father

Our Fa - ther in hea - ven, hal - lowed be your name,__ your king-dom come, your will be done, on earth as in hea - ven. Give us to - day our dai - ly bread.__ For-give us our sins as we for-give those who sin a - gainst us.__ Lead us not in-to temp-ta-tion but de - li-ver us from e - vil. For the king-dom, the pow-er, and the glo-ry are yours now and for ev - er.__ A - men.___

COPYRIGHT ADDRESSES

Permission to reproduce musical items other than those found in the Response section must be sought from:

a) the copyright holder for the music
b) the copyright holder for the words, and
c) the publisher (enquiries should be addressed to:
The Music Administrator,
HarperCollins*Religious*, 77-85 Fulham Palace Road,
London W6 8JB).

Barnard, John, c/o Jubilate Hymns, 61 Chessel Avenue, Southampton SO19 4DY

Dawney, Michael, 5 Queen's Road, Parkstone, Poole, Dorset BH14 9HF

Ferguson, Barry, Banham, 2 Hawkesdene, Shaftesbury, Dorset

Frost, David, Emerton, John, and Macintosh, Andrew, c/o The Music Administrator, HarperCollins*Religious*, 77-85 Fulham Palace Road, London W6 8JB

Hawes, Neil, 41 Burlington Road, Isleworth, Middlesex TW7 4LX

Iliff, David, c/o Jubilate Hymns, 61 Chessel Avenue, Southampton SO19 4DY

International Consultation on English Texts, c/o The Central Board of Finance of the Church of England, Church House, Great Smith Street, London SW1P 3NZ

Joint Liturgical Group, c/o The Central Board of Finance of the Church of England, Church House, Great Smith Street, London SW1P 3NZ

Llewellyn, William, c/o Oxford University Press, Walton Street, Oxford OX2 6DP

Lloyd, Richard, c/o The Music Administrator, Harpercollins*Religious*, 77-85 Fulham Palace Road, London W6 8JB

Mold, Simon, 48 Roosevelt Avenue, Chatham, Kent ME5 OEW

Rawsthorne, Noel, 23 Irby Drive, Wirral, Merseyside L61 2XL

Stephens, Howard, 17 Thornbury Avenue, Osterley, Isleworth, Middlesex TW7 4NF

Tredinnick, Noël, The All Souls' Music Office, c/o St Paul's Church, Robert Adam Street, London W1M 5AH

Warren, Norman, c/o Jubilate Hymns, 61 Chessel Avenue, Southampton SO19 4DY

White, Peter, c/o Jubilate Hymns, 61 Chessel Avenue, Southampton SO19 4DY

Wilson, David, c/o Jubilate Hymns, 61 Chessel Avenue, Southampton SO19 4DY

Index to Psalm settings

Ps 1	For the Lord cares for the way of the righteous
Ps 3	You, Lord, are about me as a shield
Ps 7	God is my shield
Ps 8	O Lord our Governor
Ps 9	I will give you thanks O Lord
Ps 10	The Lord is king for ever and ever
Ps 11	The Lord is in his holy place
Ps 15	They that do these things shall never be overthrown
Ps 16	Preserve me O God
Ps 17	Show me the wonders of your steadfast love
Ps 18	I love you O Lord my strength
Ps 19:1-6	The heavens declare the glory of God
Ps 19:7-10, 14b	The Lord is my strength and my redeemer
Ps 20	We will trust in the name of the Lord our God
Ps 22	For the kingdom is the Lord's
Ps 23	The Lord is my shepherd
Ps 24	Lift up your heads, O you gates
Ps 25	Show me your ways, O Lord
Ps 26	Lord, I love the house of your habitation
Ps 27	The Lord is my light and my salvation
Ps 28	To you will I cry, O Lord my rock
Ps 29	The Lord sits enthroned as a king for ever
Ps 30	O Lord my God I cried to you
Ps 31	Into your hand I commit my spirit
Ps 32	Blessed is he whose sin is forgiven
Ps 33	Let the whole earth fear the Lord
Ps 34	O taste and see that the Lord is good
Ps 35	Then shall my soul be joyful in the Lord
Ps 36	For with you is the well of life
Ps 37	Be still before the Lord and wait patiently for him
Ps 38	For in you Lord have I put my trust
Ps 39	I will keep watch over my ways
Ps 40	The Lord has put a new song in my mouth
Ps 42	O put your trust in God
Ps 43	O put your trust in God
Ps 45	Your throne is the throne of God
Ps 46	The Lord of hosts is with us
Ps 47	God is the king of all the earth
Ps 50	Our God is coming: he will not keep silent
Ps 51	Create in me a clean heart, O God
Ps 52	I will trust in the goodness of God for ever and ever
Ps 54	Hear my prayer O God
Ps 56	In the hour of fear: I will put my trust in you
Ps 57	Let your glory be over all the earth
Ps 61	Set me on the rock that is higher than I
Ps 62	My soul waits in silence for God
Ps 63	O God you are my God: eagerly will I seek you
Ps 65	You are to be praised O God: you that answers prayer

Ps 67	Let God be gracious to us and bless us
Ps 69	I will praise the name of God in a song
Ps 71	Great are the things that you have done
Ps 73	You will guide me with your counsel
Ps 76	Radiant in light are you
Ps 77	I call to my God and surely he will answer me
Ps 80	Show us the light of your countenance
Ps 82	Arise O God and judge the earth
Ps 84	O Lord God of hosts
Ps 85	Show us your mercy, Lord
Ps 89	Lord I will sing for ever of your loving kindnesses
Ps 90	Lord, you have been our refuge
Ps 91	The Lord himself is your refuge
Ps 92	Lord how glorious are your works
Ps 95	Come let us sing out to the Lord
Ps 97	The Lord is king: let the earth rejoice
Ps 98	O sing to the Lord a new song
Ps 100	O shout to the Lord in triumph all the earth
Ps 103	Praise the Lord, O my soul
Ps 104	Praise the Lord, my soul
Ps 105	O give thanks to the Lord and call on his name
Ps 107	O give thanks to the Lord for he is good
Ps 108	On God my heart is fixed
Ps 111	I will praise the Lord with my whole heart
Ps 112	Blessed are those who fear the Lord
Ps 113	Let the name of the Lord be blessed
Ps 114	Tremble, tremble O earth at the presence of the Lord
Ps 115	Not to us, O Lord, not to us
Ps 116	I love the Lord because he heard my voice
Ps 118	O give thanks to the Lord for he is good
Ps 119:105-107, 111,112	Your word is a lantern to my feet
Ps 119: 129-133, 135	Make your face shine upon your servant
Ps 121	The Lord himself is your keeper: the Lord is your defence
Ps 126	Those that sow in tears shall reap with songs of joy
Ps 127	Unless the Lord build the house
Ps 122	I was glad when they said to me
Ps 130	Trust in the Lord: for with him there is mercy
Ps 131	Trust in the Lord: from this time forward and for ever
Ps 133	How good and lovely it is
Ps 135	Praise the name of the Lord
Ps 139	Search me out O God and know my heart
Ps 140	O Lord my God, you are my sure stronghold
Ps 142	I call to you O Lord: I say 'You are my refuge'
Ps 145	I will exalt you O God my king
Ps 146	Praise the Lord O my soul
Ps 147	Great is the Lord and great is his power
Ps 148	Praise the Lord from heaven
Ps 149	O praise the Lord
Ps 150	Let everything that has breath praise the Lord
	Magnificat
	Nunc Dimittis
	The Easter Anthems
	Te Deum I
	Te Deum II
	Te Deum III
	Gloria in excelsis
	Bless the Lord
	Saviour of the World
	Our Father

INDEX TO PSALMS FOR THE CHURCH YEAR

Advent 1	50, 82	*Sunday after Ascension*	24, 47
Advent 2	19:1-6, 29	*Pentecost*	122, 38
Advent 3	126, Benedictus	*Trinity*	Te Deum I-III,
Advent 4	45, Magnificat		Bless the Lord
Christmas Day	98, Gloria in excelsis	*Pentecost 2*	92, 135
Christmas 1	116, 1	*Pentecost 3*	43, 69
Christmas 2	27, Nunc Dimittis	*Pentecost 4*	63, 140
Epiphany 1	36, 89	*Pentecost 5*	119, 71
Epiphany 2	100, 145	*Pentecost 6*	9, 31
Epiphany 3	46, 107	*Pentecost 7*	62, 104
9 Before Easter	103, 121	*Pentecost 8*	25, 26
8 Before Easter	147, 131	*Pentecost 9*	17, 90
7 Before Easter	32, 119	*Pentecost 10*	73, 3
Ash Wednesday	6, 51, 90	*Pentecost 11*	7, 127
Lent 1	61, 91	*Pentecost 12*	9, 133
Lent 2	40, 142	*Pentecost 13*	35, 118
Lent 3	115, 31	*Pentecost 14*	10, 80
Lent 4	18, 23	*Pentecost 15*	19, 20
Lent 5	76, 77	*Pentecost 16*	39, 108
Palm Sunday	24, 97	*Pentecost 17*	56, 57
Maundy Thursday	Saviour of the World, 3	*Pentecost 18*	52, 54
Good Friday	Saviour of the World,	*Harvest*	65, 104, 150
	130	*Pentecost 19*	61, 85
Easter Day	Easter Anthems, Te	*Pentecost 20*	42, 105
	Deum I-III, 150	*Pentecost 21*	11, 22
Easter 1	146, 34	*9 Before Christmas*	112, 148
Easter 2	23, 111	*8 Before Christmas*	113, 114
Easter 3	16, 30	*7 Before Christmas*	135, 149
Easter 4	33, 37	*6 Before Christmas*	119, 8
Easter 5	84, 15	*5 Before Christmas*	80, 147
Ascension Day	8, 95		

INDEX TO COMPOSERS AND ARRANGERS

Barnard, John Ps 47, Ps 71, Ps 150
Dawney, Michael Ps 20, Ps 28, Ps 33
Ferguson, Barry Ps 45, Ps 91, Ps 114, Ps 127
Hawes, Neil Ps 22
Iliff, David Ps 38, Ps 52, Ps 92, Ps 119:105-107, 111-112
Llewellyn, William Ps 80, Ps 89, Ps 107
Lloyd, Richard Ps 7, Ps 118, Ps 131, Ps 140
Mold, Simon Ps 18, Ps 24, Ps 27, Ps 29, Ps 39, Ps 51, Ps 67, Ps 98, Ps 105, Ps 113, Ps 116
Rawsthorne, Noel Ps 54, Ps 69, Ps 85, Ps 111, Ps 115
Stephens, Howard Ps 62, Ps 139, Ps 145
Tredinnick, Noël Ps 3, Ps 17, Ps 35

Warren, Norman Ps 8, Ps 9, Ps 11, Ps 15, Ps 16, Ps 19:1-6, 29, Ps 19:7-10, 14b, Ps 23, Ps 25, Ps 30, Ps 31, Ps 32, Ps 34, Ps 36, Ps 37, Ps 40, Ps 43, Ps 46, Ps 50, Ps 56, Ps 57, Ps 61, Ps 63, Ps 65, Ps 73, Ps 76, Ps 77, Ps 77, Ps 82, Ps 90, Ps 95, Ps 100, Ps 103, Ps 104, Ps 112, Ps 119:129-133, 135, Ps 121, Ps 122, Ps 126, Ps 130, Ps 133, Ps 135, Ps 142, Ps 146, Ps 147, Ps 148, Ps 149, Magnificat, Nunc Dimittis, The Easter Anthems, Te Deum I, Te Deum II, Te Deum III, Gloria in Excelsis, Bless the Lord, Saviour of the World, Our Father
White, Peter Ps 1, Ps 10, Ps 26, Ps 42, Ps 97, Ps 108
Wilson, David Ps 84

INDEX TO FIRST LINES

Arise O God and judge the earth — Ps 82

Be still before the Lord and wait patiently for him — Ps 37
Bless the Father, the Son and Holy Spirit — Bless the Lord
Blessed are those who fear the Lord — Ps 112
Blessed is he whose sin is forgiven — Ps 32

Christ is risen from the dead — The Easter Anthems
Come let us sing out to the Lord — Ps 95
Create in me a clean heart, O God — Ps 51

For in you Lord have I put my trust — Ps 38
For the Lord cares for the way of the righteous — Ps 1
For the kingdom is the Lord's — Ps 22
For with you is the well of life — Ps 36

Glory to God — Gloria in Excelsis
Glory to the Father — Nunc Dimittis
God is my shield — Ps 7
God is the king of all the earth — Ps 47
Great are the things that you have done — Ps 71
Great is the Lord and great is his power — Ps 147

Hear my prayer O God — Ps 54
Holy, holy, holy Lord — Te Deum I
How good and lovely it is — Ps 133

I call to my God and surely he will answer me — Ps 77
I call to you O Lord: I say 'You are my refuge — Ps 142
I love the Lord because he heard my voice — Ps 116
I love you O Lord my strength — Ps 18
I was glad when they said to me — Ps 122
I will exalt you O God my king — Ps 145
I will give you thanks O Lord — Ps 9
I will keep watch over my ways — Ps 39
I will praise the Lord with my whole heart — Ps 11
I will praise the name of God in a song — Ps 69

I will trust in the goodness of God for ever and ever — Ps 52
In the hour of fear: I will put my trust in you — Ps 56
Into your hand I commit my spirit — Ps 31

Jesus, saviour of the world — Saviour of the World

Let everything that has breath praise the Lord — Ps 150
Let God be gracious to us and bless us — Ps 67
Let the name of the Lord be blessed — Ps 113
Let the whole earth fear the Lord — Ps 33
Let your glory be over all the earth — Ps 57
Lift up your heads, O you gates — Ps 24
Lord how glorious are your works — Ps 92
Lord, I love the house of your habitation — Ps 26
Lord I will sing for ever of your loving kindnesses — Ps 89
Lord, show us your love and mercy — Te Deum III
Lord, you have been our refuge — Ps 90

Make your face shine — Ps 119:129-133, 135
My soul waits in silence for God — Ps 62

Not to us, O Lord, not to us — Ps 115

O give thanks to the Lord and call on his name — Ps 105
O give thanks to the Lord for he is good — Ps 107
O give thanks to the Lord for he is good — Ps 118
O God you are my God: eagerly will I seek you — Ps 63
O Lord God of hosts — Ps 84
O Lord my God I cried to you — Ps 30
O Lord my God, you are my sure stronghold — Ps 140
O Lord our Governor — Ps 8
O praise the Lord — Ps 149
O put your trust in God — Ps 42
O put your trust in God — Ps 43
O shout to the Lord in triumph all the earth — Ps 100
O sing to the Lord a new song — Ps 98
O taste and see that the Lord is good — Ps 34

On God my heart is fixed	Ps 108
Our Father in heaven	Our Father
Our God is coming: he will not keep silent	Ps 50
Praise the Lord from heaven	Ps 148
Praise the Lord, my soul	Ps 104
Praise the Lord, O my soul	Ps 103
Praise the Lord, O my soul	Ps 146
Praise the name of the Lord	Ps 135
Preserve me O God	Ps 16
Radiant in light are you	Ps 76
Search me out O God and know my heart	Ps 139
Set me on the rock that is higher than I	Ps 61
Show me your ways, O Lord	Ps 25
Show me the wonders of your steadfast love	Ps 17
Show us the light of your countenance	Ps 80
Show us your mercy, Lord	Ps 85
The almighty has done great things for me	Magnificat
The heavens declare the glory of God	Ps 19:1-6
The Lord is in his holy place	Ps 11
The Lord is king for ever and ever	Ps 10
The Lord is king: let the earth rejoice	Ps 97
The Lord is my light and my salvation	Ps 27

The Lord is my shepherd	Ps 23
The Lord is my strength and my redeemer	Ps 19:7-10, 14b
The Lord has put a new song in my mouth	Ps 40
The Lord himself is your keeper	Ps 121
The Lord himself is your refuge	Ps 91
The Lord of hosts is with us	Ps 46
The Lord sits enthroned as a king for ever	Ps 29
Then shall my soul be joyful in the Lord	Ps 35
They that do these things shall never be overthrown	Ps 15
Those that sow in tears shall reap with songs of joy	Ps 126
To you will I cry, O Lord my rock	Ps 28
Tremble, tremble O earth at the presence of the Lord	Ps 114
Trust in the Lord: for with him there is mercy	Ps 130
Trust in the Lord: from this time forward	Ps 131
Unless the Lord build the house	Ps 127
We will trust in the name of the Lord our God	Ps 20
You are to be praised O God	Ps 65
You, Christ, are the king of glory	Te Deum II
You, Lord, are about me as a shield	Ps 3
You will guide me with your counsel	Ps 73
Your throne is the throne of God	Ps 45
Your word is a lantern to my feet	Ps 119:105-107, 111, 112